Poetry in Medicine

Poetry in Medicine

An Anthology of Poems
About Doctors, Patients, Illness, and Healing

EDITED, WITH AN INTRODUCTION BY
MICHAEL SALCMAN

FOREWORD BY MICHAEL COLLIER

A Karen & Michael Braziller Book
PERSEA BOOKS / NEW YORK

KH

Persea Books, Inc.
277 Broadway
New York, NY 10007

Library of Congress Cataloging-in-Publication Data
Poetry in medicine : an anthology of verse about doctors, patients, illness, and healing / edited, with an introduction by Michael Salcman ; foreword by Michael Collier.
        pages cm
"A Karen & Michael Braziller book."
Summary: "Poetry in Medicine is anthology of poems written from antiquity through today about the medical experience. The book is divided into fourteen thematic sections, which present various facets of the world of medicine, doctors, and treatment. The sections include: anatomy & physiology; Contagions, Infections & Fevers; Blindness, Pain & Other Ailments; Pills, Powders & Other Remedies; Tumors, Trauma, & Tumult; From the Children's Ward; Looking Inside: Procedures, Diagnostic & Surgical; Doctors and Other Healers; Patients; The Wounded Mind: Depression & Dementia; The Final Journey: Death & Dying; The View from the Other Side of the Bed: Loved Ones of the Sick; Places of Healing; and Convalescence. It also includes a preface and introduction from anthologist, Dr. Michael Salcman, a neurosurgeon, and a foreword by poet and educator Michael Collier"—Provided by publisher.
ISBN 978-0-89255-449-2 (original trade pbk. : alk. paper)
1. Medicine—Poetry. 2. Sick--Poetry. 3. Patients—Poetry. 4. Physicians—Poetry. 5. Healing—Poetry. 6. Death—Poetry.—I. Salcman, Michael, editor. II. Title: Anthology of verse about doctors, patients, illness, and healing.
PN6110.M3P64 2015
808.81'93561—dc23
        2014023504

Designed by Rita Lascaro
Printed in the United States of America
First edition

2/23/16

CONTENTS

III.
BLINDNESS, PAIN, & OTHER AILMENTS

IV.
POWDERS, PILLS, & OTHER REMEDIES

V.
FROM THE CHILDREN'S WARD

VI.
LOOKING INSIDE: PROCEDURES, SURGICAL & DIAGNOSTIC

VII.
TUMORS, TRAUMA, & TUMULT

VIII.
DOCTORS & OTHER HEALERS

IX.

PATIENTS

X.

THE WOUNDED MIND: DEPRESSION & DEMENTIA

XI.

THE FINAL JOURNEY: DEATH & DYING

XII.

THE VIEW FROM THE OTHER SIDE OF THE BED:
LOVED ONES OF THE SICK

XIII.

HOSPITALS & OTHER PLACES OF HEALING

XIV.

CONVALESCENCE

FOREWORD

When I was invited to write the foreword for Michael Salcman's *Poetry in Medicine*, which at the time I knew only by title, one of the things that came to mind was "The Gross Clinic," Thomas Eakins' large, magnificent painting depicting a nineteenth-century surgical theater. It is so famous I probably don't need to remind you that at the center of the painting stands the surgeon Samuel Gross holding a scalpel in his bloodied right hand. He has turned away from the patient whose open incision is being retracted by one assistant while being probed with an instrument by another. There are many remarkable things about this painting, including the gallery of shadowy medical students many of whom appear to be indifferently attentive or even asleep, as well as the image of a woman, thought to be the patient's mother, shielding herself from the scene in melodramatic horror. And you don't have to look closely at Gross, or for long, to begin to get the idea that Eakins might want you to consider the possibility that Gross is an artist, a painter like him.

Well, it is after all a painting, so why not have the surgeon be a stand-in for the artist? It's a fair analogy, except most painters are careful not to get paint on their hands. Not so the surgeon. The surgeon by necessity has visceral contact with the medium, which is flesh and blood. But Gross is an actor in the drama of the operation he has set in motion, not an observer of it, not the way the artist is. The artist is the one who notices the patient's feet are covered in gray socks, a detail that seems of little significance. He notices as well the more obvious detail of the patient's head hidden beneath a wad of chloroform-soaked cotton. You might say that the subtle arrangement and alignment of these details by Eakins is a form of poetry in medicine.

As I began considering Michael Salcman's anthology, I didn't know if Eakins' painting would be relevant to my experience of reading it but I very quickly came to see that the painting contained features common to the anthology. Eakins' realism characterizes many of the poems. There's Philip Larkin's "Faith Healing" ("Slowly the women file to where he stands/ Upright in rimless glasses, silver hair,/ Dark suit, white collar.")

and Edward Hirsch's "Blunt Morning" ("She was breathing heavily, she was laboring/ in her non-sleep, in her state of drifting// to wherever she was going."). And much frightening and graphic detail, the way we see it in Salcman's own "The Apprentice Surgeon" ("How awful for him to cut the flesh or watch/ a deep cut made before carbolic acid,/ before ether . . . "). There are even the beginnings of the medicalization of healing found in Bob Hicok's "Surgery" ("How else can it be/ for strangers who take your breath,/ contain it in a machine and give it back,/ its meter undisturbed."

While "The Gross Clinic" provided a rich starting place for thinking about the relationship of art and medicine there is a vital element missing from it. Gross, who wears a countenance of grave triumphalism, seems to hold the patient in disdain or disgust. We might as well be witnessing an autopsy for all we are asked to feel for the patient. Even the patient's mother so horrified by what is happening, turns away and covers her eyes. She can't bear to look because her son is more like a specimen or a subject of a medical or science experiment than an individual person.

In contrast to the tradition in Eakins' painting that elevates physicians above patients, Michael Salcman has assembled in *Poetry in Medicine*, a collection of poems that puts humans and humanity at the center of its concern. And if the poems alone didn't make this clear, Salcman's decision to put Eakins' "The Agnew Clinic" on the cover only underscores his commitment to this ethic. Salcman, who is a distinguished neurosurgeon, reminds us in the first sentence of his preface that "all of us are born as patients," and this crucial, humane idea remains a touchstone throughout the book. The mystery of our existence as experienced through sickness, healing, and death, and through the inexorable failings of the body, is what Salcman illuminates again and again in his selection and ordering of the poems. The ill and the wounded and the wound dresser, to borrow an image from Whitman, are the inescapable roles all of us must play, and *Poetry in Medicine*, showcases rich and compelling examples of these.

As a doctor and poet, Salcman is naturally drawn to poems about medicine and after decades of gathering them, he has fashioned a definitive collection that records the widest possible range of human responses to the predicament of mortality. Most of the poems are written from the patient's point of view or from the point of view of the patient's friends and family. A number are by familiar doctor poets such as John Keats,

William Carlos Williams and others by less familiar physicians such as Dannie Abse, Gottfried Benn, and Miroslav Holub. The tonal range of the poems is as various as our experience of, yes, life: humorous, angry, fearful, resigned, impatient, and imploring. Some of the most moving poems Salcman has gathered are those written in extremis, such as Jason Shinder's profoundly clarifying final poems and Marie Howe's record of her brother's succumbing to AIDS. Sometimes the poems are not about illness at all but as in Linda Pastan's "At The Gynecologist," they confront the scarily provisional nature of health; how at times we can seem to be a doctor's visit away from very bad news. One of my favorites is Daniel Hoffman's "A Triumph," an ironically poignant elegy about the death of his pediatrician father.

In a collection as compendious as *Poetry in Medicine*, it is difficult to completely describe the territory covered but Salcman shrinks it for the reader by providing many thematic points of access. His decision to gather poems about convalescence at the end of the book gives the reader a lift and it speaks to the courage, endurance, and hope guiding the overall project. While *Poetry in Medicine* contains poems from the Western Tradition as early as Ovid, a great many are from the past century and a half and are written in a colloquial free verse. Many great poets from the Tradition—Shakespeare, Donne, Milton, Dickinson—are represented, of course, but one of the particular pleasures in reading the anthology is encountering lesser-known poets such as Sarah Cross, another doctor poet, among many others.

If the power of Eakins' portrait of Samuel Gross derives from having the surgeon at the center of the drama, providing only scant space for the utterly human detail of the patient's sock-covered feet, Salcman's *Poetry in Medicine* does the opposite. By featuring poems that put the human individual at the center as either speaker or subject, he has created an intensely intimate experience of what it means to face mortality, one that gains power by being deeply personal. What I mean by personal is that we come to see these poems and their arrangement are not merely an anthology. They also represent the vision of a particular man, doctor and poet Michael Salcman, whose vocations have come together seamlessly in *Poetry in Medicine* to provide all of us patients with an intricate, sometimes terrifying, sometimes reassuring, map to the precariousness of life.

—Michael Collier

PREFACE

All of us are born as patients, we carry within us the sources of and susceptibilities to major and minor disruptions of our physical and emotional vitality and those of you holding this volume are among the many readers of literary creations in which issues surrounding health and illness, doctors and diseases play a major and dramatic role. Like most of you I was a reader before I became a writer and like a few I was a poet before I became a doctor. I was also caught in the last major polio outbreak when I was five years old and this experience was definitive in determining my choice of a medical career. As a bed-bound child I read poems and stories by Edgar Allen Poe, novels by Sinclair Lewis, and Arthur Conan Doyle's transcriptions of notes made by Dr. John Watson, the amanuensis of Sherlock Holmes. Much later I would run across especially powerful poems on medical themes and place them in a drawer for later use, poems by Emily Dickinson and Walt Whitman from the nineteenth century and more modernist offerings by William Carlos Williams and Anne Sexton. It soon became clear that the number and power of literary works devoted to medical themes had grown in parallel with the development of modern medicine, the imaginative works and their subjects sharing a similar historical arc. Moreover, the dominant topic covered by poems and stories in any particular era appeared to be determined by the most important public health problem of the time; in almost every case this usually turned out be the major infectious disease or contagion of the time. Thereafter the same medical condition was often used as a powerful metaphor for other issues; Blake's "Sick Rose" and Poe's "Masque of The Red Death" conjoin contagion with moral weakness and spiritual illness. These historical observations are the main themes of the introductory essay, a chronological presentation of parallel developments in poetry and medicine.

In contrast to the Introduction, the poems in this book are thematically organized in such a way as to facilitate access to subjects of particular interest to the reader, whether patient, friend or parent, medical student, surgeon or pediatrician, nurse or minister. This thematic structure collects poems on a variety of topics including surgical and non-surgical ailments and treatments, the separate perspectives of patients, doctors and loved ones, voices from the children's ward and poems about places of healing and recovery. By this method similarities of human experience down through the ages become apparent, whether the speaker of the poem is facing an older contagion like tuberculosis or a more contemporary problem such as AIDS, whether the patient's mind has been wounded by drink and depression or by the newer public health scourge of Alzheimer's disease. This anthology of poems about illness, patients and healers is meant to be unique in a number of other ways. It is purposely historical in nature, gathering together the best poems on the subject by the widest array of significant voices in the Western canon; it specifically does not emphasize poetry by physician-writers and does not restrict itself to contemporary work. It deals much more extensively than previous anthologies with diseases of the body rather than those of the mind, the latter a favorite preoccupation of the confessional poets of fifty years ago. Many poets have written about illness, hospitals and healers out of their direct experience as patients or as the loved ones of patients, others because of their service as nurses (Whitman) or physicians (W. C. Williams), a few have been devoted to the subject for more obscure reasons (Auden); the reader will find some of these matters clarified in the brief biographies that conclude the book.

INTRODUCTION:
Poetry about Doctors and Diseases

Let us go then, you and I,
When the evening is spread out against the sky
Like a patient etherised upon a table . . .
>   —from "The Love Song of J. Alfred Prufrock"
>   by T. S. Eliot

No lover of imaginative writing or poetry should be surprised about the voluminous literature on doctors and diseases. Illness is a universal human experience, almost as certain as death, taxes, and romantic disappointment, and one's response to it is often a mix of normal concern, perplexity, fear, and false bravado, occasionally leavened with philosophical reflection. Some of history's most profound poems are responses to the pain and suffering of others, the foibles and heroics of physicians and care-givers, the nature of illness and the wisdom of the body. Keats was 22 years old and nursing his brother Tom when he sent a letter to J.H. Reynolds in which he said, "Until we are sick, we understand not;—in fine, as Byron says, 'Knowledge is Sorrow'; and I go on to say that 'Sorrow is Wisdom'." The drama of the sick room has been the subject of much poetry.

Perhaps the best of this literature developed during the past two centuries, *para passu* with the evolution of the modern hospital and the surgical operating theater. But the advent of scientific medicine did not remove the almost surrealistic fear and mystery felt by the general public about the workings of the body; in some cases, it served to intensify it. The introduction of general anesthesia in the mid-nineteenth century exposed patients to a new and not necessarily pleasant means of unconsciously letting go. The opening lines of Eliot's *Prufrock*, above, reflect this.

At the start of the Western poetic canon (c. 800 BCE), when both the Hebrew Bible and the Homeric epics were codified, doctors and diseases are present only to a circumscribed degree. In *The Iliad*, Homer mentions 150 different wounds, and explains with some degree of anatomical accuracy why some are fatal; spears and arrows strike specific internal organs according to entry point and trajectory. Although the Hebrew Bible mentions a variety of diseases and their treatments, no physicians are named. The ten plagues in Exodus are described with poetic concision, and at least four involve possible medical ailments: infestation by lice, a livestock epidemic similar to anthrax, painful boils, and the death of the first-born. For treatment the Bible mentions a relatively limited number of salves and medications.

Other classical texts include Ovid's *Medicamina Faciei Femineae* or *The Art of Beauty*, the final half of which contains five complete recipes for cosmetics and dermatological treatments guaranteed to cure blackheads, pimples, wrinkles, and spots. Ovid's close contemporary, Virgil, the author of the *Georgics* and the *Aeneid*, studied medicine, philosophy, and poetry. Other polymaths include Yehuda Halevi, Spanish philosopher-physician and the finest poet of the Golden Age in Iberia prior to the Jewish expulsion, and Dante, author of the *Vita Nuova*, who started out on a political career by inscribing himself in the guild of physicians and apothecaries. In the *Commedia* he rarely mentions physicians, and then usually because of their importance as philosophers. Except for Michael Scot, a physician and astrologer, the medical figures in the *Inferno* are found in the First Circle (limbo), either because they lived in the pre-Christian era or in non-Christian lands without benefit of baptism (Accardo).

The Plague

Until recent times, infectious diseases were the most important causes of death and disability; therefore, the great epidemics and contagions provide a useful scaffold upon which to hang the history of poetry in medicine. The first detailed description of Bubonic Plague (1351) is found in the one hundred stories of Giovanni Boccaccio's masterpiece, *The Decameron*, itself a possible source for several of the stories in Chaucer's *Canterbury Tales*. Boccaccio opens his book with a wide-ranging description of the Bubonic Plague including its physical, psychological, and social effects. His reportage is remarkable because the Black Death had only very recently arrived in Europe (c. 1347), probably from Asia, most likely as an invisible immigrant accompanying gangs of slaves and laborers delivering bales of Chinese silk at a Black Sea port (Ascherson). Between December 1347 and September 1348, the Black Death killed three-quarters of the European population in the Crimea and half the population of Venice. In 1563, 20,000 Londoners died of the disease.

Thomas Campion, an early Renaissance poet and physician, probably died in one of the first Bubonic Plague outbreaks. Much later, and much like Boccaccio's refugees, Sir Isaac Newton was driven to the countryside where he saw the apple fall; plague was raging in his home city and Cambridge University was closed for almost two years. Petrarch, a friend of Boccaccio, lost at least one child to the Plague and was so exorcised about the limited knowledge available to medieval physicians that he devoted the first of his four *Invectives* to an argument on behalf of the Humanities against Medicine. Petrarch's skepticism was shared by Chaucer, who included a physician as one of his pilgrims in *The Canterbury Tales.* It is thought that Chaucer, in the course of his governmental duties, met both Petrarch and Boccaccio. Chaucer's physician, clad in taffeta, bases his practice on a thorough understanding of astrology and the four humors. The later foundations of scientific medicine depended as much on a proper understanding of the body, its anatomy and physiology, as it did on an understanding of disease, but in most of Christian Europe at that time, it was not possible to carry out human autopsies.

Shakespeare was intimately familiar with Bubonic Plague; he lost three sisters to the disease, his brother Edmund, and his son Hamnet, who was only eleven. As Michael Cummings writes, "[London] at that time was a prolific breeding ground of disease because of crowded, unsanitary conditions. Garbage littered the streets. Residents emptied chamber pots out windows. Brothels incubated syphilis. Dung clotted gutters and waterways. Flies and rodents carried bacteria and viruses from one section of the city to another.... Even the queen bathed only once a month." Special officials called "searchers" were empowered to enter and search houses for possible victims and were paid to enforce quarantine. In *Romeo and Juliet*, Friar John, suspected of having plague, is shut up in a house by the searchers; this action prevents him from delivering a critical message from Friar Lawrence to Romeo, with tragic consequences. Outbreaks of plague caused the London theaters to be shut down in 1593, 1603, 1608, and again in 1665.

In his plays, Shakespeare makes reference to a large number of other diseases, including scurvy, gout, epilepsy, rheumatism, and venereal disease, as well as several varieties of madness. Syphilis, first coined as a medical term in 1530, appears as the pox in 10 of Shakespeare's plays. In *Julius Caesar* (1599), Act I, Scene 2, Cassius, Casca, and Brutus discuss the possibility that Caesar suffers from "the falling sickness" or epilepsy;

Shakespeare's accurate description of a seizure is turned into a pun for political weakness:

> CASSIUS
> But, soft, I pray you: what, did Caesar swound?
> CASCA
> He fell down in the market-place, and foamed at
> mouth, and was speechless.
> BRUTUS
> 'Tis very like: he hath the falling sickness.
> CASSIUS
> No, Caesar hath it not; but you and I,
> And honest Casca, we have the falling sickness.

In the plays, his portrayals of various forms of psychopathology, madness, and depression in *King Lear*, *Macbeth*, *Hamlet*, and *Coriolanus* are beyond compare. On the other hand Shakespeare's sonnets rarely refer to medical matters except as metaphors.

Given the ineffectiveness and risk of medical treatment in this era, not to mention the pomposity of some practitioners, physicians became frequent objects of dramatic fun and literary satire, as in Moliere's comedies. John Dryden, a master of satiric verse, frequently chose physicians as his targets; his apothegms remain a staple of holistic web sites: *Insanity: doing the same thing over and over again and expecting different results* (from *The Spanish Fryar* (Act II, Sc.1), 1681). The tendency towards satire is also reflected in eighteenth and nineteenth century nursery rhymes, where one encounters sly criticism of the doctor's self-importance. On the other hand, the death of a physician occasioned a heart-felt encomium by Samuel Johnson, who wrote in praise of his recently deceased friend Dr. Levet:

> When fainting nature call'd for aid,
> And hov'ring death prepar'd the blow,
> His vig'rous remedy display'd
> The power of art without the show.

Early physician-poets writing in English, like the aforementioned Thomas Campion, did not often write about their medical experiences. This was true of Arthur Johnson, a Scot, who studied medicine in Padua and wrote a version of the Psalms in Latin; and Henry Vaughan, a Welsh physician and mystical poet. University-trained physicians more often turned to religious verse, as happened with Vaughan, especially after his conversion.

Tuberculosis

Known as "consumption" or "the wasting disease," tuberculosis, like the plague before it, was spread by crowding and the unsanitary conditions of modern urban centers; this truly gruesome and almost invariably fatal illness further exposed the general ineffectiveness of medicine as practiced prior to the mid-nineteenth century. John Keats, the greatest of all physician-poets, trained as an apprentice surgeon or apothecary but never practiced and rarely spoke of his own experience with the illness, except to close friends and in his letters; the poems are nearly devoid of references to hospital and disease. In the "infamous" Blackwoods review of *Endymion*, the young poet was advised to return to his former occupation: "It is a better and wiser thing to be a starved apothecary than a starved poet. So back to the shop, Mr. John, back to 'plasters, pills and etc"

When Keats first coughed up bright arterial blood, he knew enough medicine to quickly realize he would die of consumption. His doctors, supposedly expert in the treatment of tuberculosis, one and all ascribed his wasting illness to a combination of melancholia and stomach disorder, and further compounded his difficulties by bleeding and starving him. A particularly grim description of blood-letting by a ship's surgeon is found in Byron's *Don Juan*:

> He but requested to be bled to death:
> The surgeon had his instruments, and bled
> Pedrillo, and so gently ebb'd his breath,
> You hardly could perceive when he was dead.
> He died as born, a Catholic in faith,
> Like most in the belief in which they're bred,
> And first a little crucifix he kiss'd,
> And then held out his jugular and wrist.

Keats, in his various roles as nurse, physician, writer, and patient, was all-too familiar with the status of medical practice at this time (Plumly). His close experience with the bare facts of existence as displayed in the autopsy room and operating theater must have conditioned his development as a poet. He watched his mother die of consumption and nursed his younger brother Tom through the final months of the illness. In his revised version of *Hyperion*, Keats joined his two professions in an admirable example of negative capability. Here, the Poet is speaking to the muse Moneta:

> Majestic shadow, tell me: sure not all
> Those melodies sung into the world's ear
> Are useless: sure a poet is a sage;
> A humanist, physician to all men.

Other Romantic poets had close knowledge of medical subjects and the primitive pharmacopeia. Friedrich Schiller trained as a physician and spent most of his life mistakenly attempting to treat his own illnesses; in this he was notably less successful than he was in his literary pursuits.

Typhus, Typhoid, Cholera, and Dysentery

During wartime in the nineteenth century, new epidemics appeared; cholera and typhus rivaled tuberculosis as a cause of illness and death. Adam Mickiewicz (1798–1855), the national poet of Poland and one of the founders of Romanticism, died of cholera in Constantinople, organizing troops to fight against the Russians in the Crimean War. Ten times as many soldiers died from typhus, typhoid, cholera,and dysentery as were lost to battle wounds. Gerard Manley Hopkins died of typhoid fever while working in the slums of Dublin.

The public's general opinion of hospitals was not much better than their view of most physicians. The hospital was seen as a place of suffering, infection, and death; in *Paris Spleen*, Baudelaire used the hospital to exemplify helplessness: "Life is a hospital in which each patient is possessed by the desire to change his bed." Constantine Cavafy, who spent his life in Alexandria living above a brothel with a clear view of a church and the gardens of the Greek Hospital, put it this way: "Where could I live better? Below, the brothel caters to the flesh. And there is the church which forgives sin. And there is the hospital where we die."

The majority of hospital nursing continued to be given by family members and volunteers. Walt Whitman, who had no medical training, served as a volunteer nurse during the Civil War and wrote eloquently about the value of tender, loving care in the treatment of injured soldiers. His first collection, *Drum Taps*, and several essays fully describe his experience.

In the nineteenth century, the best poems about medicine and illness were written by non-physicians, professional poets who kept body, soul, and home together by engaging in other avocations: pastor, lawyer, banker, editor, private person and public scold. Both Emily Dickinson and Walt Whitman devoted a number of poems to medical subjects such as melancholia and grief and grieving. Towards the end of the nineteenth century, the increasing professionalization of medicine and the elaboration of its scientific method allowed some writer-physicians to support their artistic pursuits through active and prolonged medical practice. In a letter to a friend, Anton Chekhov, who spent seven years working in a tuberculosis sanitarium, described his dual-career in the following manner:

> Medicine is my lawful wife, and literature is my mistress.
> When I get fed up with one, I spend the night with the other.
> Though it is irregular, it is less boring this way, and besides,
> neither of them loses anything through my infidelity.

The Victorian author of "Invictus," William Ernest Henley, developed tuberculosis in his legs and underwent amputation at age 25; he was perhaps the first to devote a sequence of poems to a medical subject, *In Hospital*. Written from the perspective of a patient, the poems in his collection, *A Book of Verses*, are realistic in tone. One of the poems, most of which are sonnet variants, is a description of his doctor, Joseph Lister, the father of antisepsis.

More Recent Plagues

During the twentieth century, other contagions and wasting diseases have come to occupy the metaphoric space tuberculosis and consumption previously filled. In World War I, not all of the famous British poets who died were killed on the battlefield. Rupert Brooke died of sepsis from an infected mosquito bite on his way to Gallipoli. Wilfred Owen famously wrote, "My subject is War, and the pity of War. The poetry is in the pity."

The war was followed by an outbreak of viral encephalitis (influenza) that left many of its survivors with late-onset Parkinson's disease. Typhus and typhoid make their appearance in numerous poems and memoirs about the European concentration camps and the prisons of the Gulag. Anne Frank and her sister died of louse-borne typhus at Bergen-Belsen, as did Robert Desnos, the French surrealist poet, who died at Terezín two days after liberation. During the German occupation, two Polish poets, Jerzy Hordynski and Zbigniew Herbert, actually worked as "lice-feeders" at Rudolf Weigl's Institute of Typhus Studies. Anna Akhmatova became seriously ill with typhus after her evacuation from Leningrad in 1941; as a young woman she had already suffered with tuberculosis and chronic bronchitis. Freud's writings in the early twentieth century increased general frankness about the body and psychological processes. Profound attention to the interior mental life of literary characters became a commonplace in the poetry of Thomas Hardy, Robert Frost, and Wallace Stevens.

William Carlos Williams, a central member of the pioneering Modernist generation, remained a practicing physician all his life and wrote many of his poems while making his rounds in Paterson, New Jersey. His manner of gathering experience about the self in the sick room probably informed "The World Contracted to a Recognizable Image," one of his more mysterious poems with a medical reference, almost certainly about an illness of his own.

Some of the early European Modernists were also physicians, including Gottfried Benn, a major exponent of German expressionism; Miroslav Holub, equally famous as immunologist and poet; and Dannie Abse, a British pulmonologist and eminent writer of plays, memoirs, and poems. Paul Celan briefly studied medicine before majoring in literature. More recent physician-writers have followed the lead of Williams, Holub, and Abse, fully pursuing joint careers in medicine and poetry. The devotion of Williams to both poetry and medicine exemplified the ideals put forth by W.H. Auden, himself the son of a physician:

"A doctor, like anyone else who has to deal with human beings, each of them unique, cannot be a scientist: he is either, like the surgeon, a craftsman, or, like the physician and the psychologist, an artist. This means that in order to be a good doctor a man must also have a good character, that is to say, whatever weaknesses and foibles he may have, he must", as W.H. Auden wrote, "love his fellow human beings in the concrete and desire their good before his own."

Mental Illness, Breast Cancer, and HIV

In the late twentieth century, the rise of identity art in all media, that is to say artistic production based on the membership of its creator in a particular social group, produced a great flowering of powerful and well-informed poems devoted to subjects of special interest. The high incidence of mental illness, alcoholism, suicide, and depression in this generation of poets has been the subject of frequent comment: Elizabeth Bishop, Robert Lowell, Sylvia Plath, Anne Sexton, Delmore Schwartz, Theodore Roethke, and John Berryman all suffered from a variety of such conditions. The black dog of despond is rarely coded in their work but, as Adam Kirsch points out, their purpose in writing of it and other disturbing matters was not confession but aesthetics.

Kirsch uses *The Wounded Surgeon*, the title of his study, as a new and more suitable metaphor for the heroic stance of poets in subjecting their most intimate concerns to the objective fire of art. The metaphor comes from Eliot's "East Coker": "The wounded surgeon plies the steel/ That questions the distempered part."

Poets such as Alicia Ostriker, Lucille Clifton, and Marilyn Hacker have movingly written of body image and the impact of breast cancer on self-esteem and personal relationships. References to the details of surgical procedures, modern diagnostic techniques, and theories of pathophysiology have entered the poet's vocabulary. Thom Gunn, David Bergman, Alfred Corn, and Mark Doty have explicitly documented the horrors of HIV-related illnesses. Poems devoted to HIV are in the long tradition of poems about contagious and infectious illnesses, including the Black Plague, tuberculosis, typhus, polio, and the influenza pandemic.

Our latest epidemic, that of Alzheimer's disease and related dementias, is an unintended consequence of the increased longevity conferred by the recent successes and triumphs of modern medicine, a public health crisis movingly addressed by Rachel Hadas, C. K. Williams, and other poets. They provide ample evidence that doctors and diseases remain central and compelling subjects in contemporary poetry.

Bibliography

Pasquale Accardo: Dante and Medicine: The Circle of Malpractice, Southern Medical Journal, 82(5): 624–628, 1989

Neal Ascherson: *Black Sea*, Hill and Wang, New York, 1996, pp. 95–96

Michael J. Cummings: *Shakespeare and Medicine*, 2010, http://www.cummingsstudyguides.net/xMedicine.html

Adam Kirsch: *The Wounded Surgeon*, Confession and Transformation in Six American Poets, Norton, New York, 2005

Stanley Plumly: *Posthumous Keats*, Norton, New York, 2008

William Carlos Williams: *The Practice* (from The Doctor Stories, New Directions, 1951), reprinted in American Poetry Review 38(6):29–30, November/December, 2009

Poetry in Medicine

I.

THE WISDOM OF THE BODY: ANATOMY & PHYSIOLOGY

James Merrill (1926–1995)

b o d y

Look closely at the letters. Can you see,
entering (stage right), then floating full,
then heading off—so soon—
how like a little kohl-rimmed moon
o plots her course from *b* to *d*

—as *y*, unanswered, knocks at the stage door?
Looked at too long, words fail,
phase out. Ask, now that *body* shines
no longer, by what light you learn these lines
and what the *b* and *d* stood for.

LES MURRAY (b. 1938)

Cell DNA

I am the singular
in free fall.
I and my doubles
carry it all:

life's slim volume
spirally bound.
It's what I'm about,
it's what I'm around.

Presence and hungers
imbue a sap mote
with the world as they spin it.
I teach it by rote

but its every command
was once a miscue
that something rose to,
Presence and freedom

re-wording, re-beading
strains on a strand
making I and I more different
than we could stand.

BRENDAN GALVIN (b. 1938)

Fear of *Gray's Anatomy*

I will not look in it again.
There the heart in section is a gas mask,
its windows gone, its hoses severed.
The spinal cord is a zipper
& the lower digestive tract
has been squeezed from a tube like toothpaste.
All my life I had hoped someday to own
at least myself, only to find I am
Flood's ligaments, the areola of Mamma,
& zonule of Zinn. Ruffini's endings
end in me, & the band of Gennari lies near
the island of Reil. Though I am a geography
greater than even I surmised, containing as I do
spaces & systems, promontories & at least
one reservoir, pits, tunnels, crescents,
demilunes & a daughter star, how can I celebrate
my incomplete fissures, my hippocampus &
inferior mental processes, my depressions
& internal extremities? I encompass also
ploughshare & gladiolus, iris & wing,
& the bird's nest of my cerebellum,
yet wherever I go I bear the crypts of Lieberkühn,
& among the possible malfunctionaries,
floating ribs & wandering cells, Pott's fracture,
mottles, abductors, lachrymal bones & aberrant ducts.
I will ask my wife to knot a jacket for this book,
& pretend it's a brick doorstop.
I will not open *Gray's Anatomy* again.

KIMBERLY JOHNSON (b. 1971)

Ode on My Belly Button

My original wound was my deepest:
half-inch divot where the cord shriveled off
and a plunging ache that never scabbed
where my umbilical name sloughed away,—
forgotten now, but it meant *Belong.* Whole
again and joyful when my ninth-month
belly swelled with genial weight, skin taut,
fullest at the center line where fragile
the navel flattened out, its secret flesh
splayed to surface, until my familiar
agony: headlong and vulnerable,
our mutual attachment already
obsolescing, you inherit your original wound.
                    —Your original loneliness.

Sʏʟᴠɪᴀ Pʟᴀᴛʜ (1932–1963)

Two Views of a Cadaver Room

1

The day she visited the dissecting room
They had four men laid out, black as burnt turkey,
Already half unstrung. A vinegary fume
Of the death vats clung to them;
The white-smocked boys started working.
The head of his cadaver had caved in,
And she could scarcely make out anything
In that rubble of skull plates and old leather.
A sallow piece of string held it together.

In their jars the snail-nosed babies moon and glow.
He hands her the cut-out heart like a cracked heirloom.

2

In Brueghel's panorama of smoke and slaughter
Two people only are blind to the carrion army:
He, afloat in the sea of her blue satin
Skirts, sings in the direction
Of her bare shoulder, while she bends,
Fingering a leaflet of music, over him,
Both of them deaf to the fiddle in the hands
Of the death's-head shadowing their song.
These Flemish lovers flourish; not for long.

Yet desolation, stalled in paint, spares the little country
Foolish, delicate, in the lower right-hand corner.

RICHARD WILBUR (b. 1921)

To His Skeleton

Why will you vex me with
These bone-spurs in the ear,
With X-rayed phlebolith
And calculus? See here,

Noblest of armatures,
The grin which bares my teeth
Is mine as yet, not yours.
Did you not stand beneath

This flesh, I could not stand,
But would revert to slime
Informous and unmanned;
And I may come in time

To wish your peace my fate,
Your sculpture my renown.
Still, I have held you straight
And mean to lay you down

Without too much disgrace
When what can perish dies.
For now then, keep your place
And do not colonize.

Jane Hirshfield (b. 1953)

A Hand

A hand is not four fingers and a thumb.

Nor is it palm and knuckles,
not ligaments or the fat's yellow pillow,
not tendons, star of the wristbone, meander of veins.

A hand is not the thick thatch of its lines
with their infinite dramas,
nor what it has written,
not on the page,
not on the ecstatic body.

Nor is the hand its meadows of holding, of shaping—
not sponge of rising yeast-bread,
not rotor pin's smoothness,
not ink.

The maple's green hands do not cup
the proliferant rain.
What empties itself falls into the place that is open.

A hand turned upward holds only a single, transparent question.

Unanswerable, humming like bees, it rises, swarms, departs.

DAVID BERGMAN (b. 1950)

My Father's Penis

A nurse removes from my father a Foley
catheter through which like an hourglass
the liquid sands of urine have dripped.
But just as it's out, he starts to bleed
and suddenly the room is full of women.
I, who have stood in the doorway, now turn
to see what they are doing: a blond carefully
swabs his genitals, and the large,
black nurse, whose face is a mask of fat,
places a towel beneath his groin. I hide
my eyes, afraid, not of the blood,
but of the soft, gray thing between his legs.
Later my father quips: I had to wait
until ninety to be surrounded by girls
all looking with interest at my penis.

STEPHEN DUNN (b. 1939)

The Routine Things Around the House

When Mother died
I thought: now I'll have a death poem.
That was unforgivable

yet I've since forgiven myself
as sons are able to do
who've been loved by their mothers.

I stared into the coffin
knowing how long she'd live,
how many lifetimes there are

in the sweet revisions of memory.
It's hard to know exactly
how we ease ourselves back from sadness,

but I remembered when I was twelve,
1951, before the world
unbuttoned its blouse.

I had asked my mother (I was trembling)
if I could see her breasts
and she took me into her room

without embarrassment or coyness
and I stared at them,
afraid to ask for more.

Now, years later, someone tells me
Cancers who've never had mother love
are doomed and I, a Cancer,

feel blessed again. What luck
to have had a mother
who showed me her breasts

when girls my age were developing
their separate countries,
what luck

she didn't doom me
with too much or too little.
Had I asked to touch,

perhaps to suck them,
what would she have done?
Mother, dead woman

who I think permits me
to love women easily,
this poem

is dedicated to where
we stopped, to the incompleteness
that was sufficient

and to how you buttoned up,
began doing the routine things
around the house.

CLAUDIA EMERSON (1957–2014)

Anatomical Model

They have retired her, alongside turtles'
shells, bees' nests, and the skeletons of birds,

to a narrow glass closet. She is antique
but not inaccurate—headless, armless,

all torso, a sculpture mutilated. The breast
lifts off, easy as the lid from a pot, the heart

and lungs beneath; the belly comes away then
from neat intestines, from the chalky fetus nestled

in the womb worn smooth from all the hands
reaching in for this conclusion.

JOHN STONE (1936–2008)

Cadaver

"The initial lesion of syphilis may result over the years in a gradual weakening and dilatation (aneurysm) of the aorta. This aneurysm may ultimately rupture and lead to death of the patient."
    —Medical Textbook

Fitting the labels
in our books
to our own tense tendons
slipping in their sheaths

we memorized the body
and the word

stripped the toughened skin
from the stringing nerve
the giving muscle.

Ribs sprang like gates.

In the chest
like archaeologists
we found it:
clotted, swollen,
aneurysmal
sign of an old sin—

the silent lust
that had buried itself
in the years

growing
in the hollow of his chest

still rounded by her arms
clinging
belly to belly
years beyond that first seed

to the rigid final fact

of a body.

Thomas James (1946–1974)

Mummy of a Lady Named Jemutesonekh XXI Dynasty

My body holds its shape. The genius is intact.
Will I return to Thebes? In that lost country
The eucalyptus trees have turned to stone.
Once, branches nudged me, dropping swollen blossoms,
And passionflowers lit my father's garden.
Is it still there, that place of mottled shadow,
The scarlet flowers breathing in the darkness?

I remember how I died. It was so simple!
One morning the garden faded. My face blacked out.
On my left side they made the first incision.
They washed my heart and liver in palm wine—
My lungs were two dark fruit they stuffed with spices.
They smeared my innards with a sticky unguent
And sealed them in a crock of alabaster.

My brain was next. A pointed instrument
Hooked it through my nostrils, strand by strand.
A voice swayed over me. I paid no notice
For weeks my body swam in sweet perfume.
I came out scoured. I was skin and bone.
They lifted me into the sun again
And packed my empty skull with cinnamon.

They slit my toes; a razor gashed my fingertips
Stitched shut at last, my limbs were chaste and valuable,
Stuffed with paste of cloves and wild honey.
My eyes were empty, so they filled them up,
Inserting little nuggets of obsidian.
A basalt scarab wedged between my breast
Replaced the tinny music of my heart.

Hands touched my sutures. I was so important!
They oiled my pores, rubbing a fragrance in.
An amber gum oozed down to soothe my temples.
I wanted to sit up. My skin was luminous,
Frail as the shadow of an emerald.
Before I learned to love myself too much,
My body wound itself in spools of linen.

Shut in my painted box, I am a precious object.
I wear a wooden mask. These are my eyelids,
Two flakes of bronze, and here is my new mouth,
Chiseled with care, guarding its ruby facets.
I will last forever. I am not impatient—
My skin will wait to greet its old complexions.
I'll lie here till the world swims back again.

When I come home the garden will be budding,
White petals breaking open, clusters of night flowers,
The far-off music of a tambourine.
A boy will pace among the passionflowers,
His eyes no longer two bruised surfaces.
I'll know the mouth of my young groom, I'll touch
His hands. Why do people lie to one another?

William Matthews (1942–1997)

Eyes:

the only parts of the body the same
size at birth as they'll always be.
"That's why all babies are beautiful,"
Thurber used to say as he grew
blind—not dark, he'd go on
to explain, but floating in a pale
light always, a kind of candlelit
murk from a sourceless light.
He needed dark to see:
for a while he drew on black
paper with white pastel chalk
but it grew worse. Light bored
into his eyes but where did it go?
Into a sea of phosphenes,
along the wet fuse of some dead
nerve, it hid everywhere and couldn't
be found. I've used up
three guesses, all of them
right. It's like scuba diving, going down
into the black cone-tip that dives
farther than I can, though I dive
closer all the time.

DANNIE ABSE (b. 1923)

Pathology of Colours

I know the colour rose, and it is lovely,
but not when it ripens in a tumour;
and healing greens, leaves and grass, so springlike,
in limbs that fester are not springlike.

I have seen red-blue tinged with hirsute mauve
in the plum-skin face of a suicide.
I have seen white, china white almost, stare
from behind the smashed windscreen of a car.

And the criminal, multi-coloured flash
of an H-bomb is no more beautiful
than an autopsy when the belly's opened—
to show cathedral windows never opened.

So in the simple blessing of a rainbow,
in the bevelled edge of a sunlit mirror,
I have seen, visible, Death's artefact
like a soldier's ribbon on a tunic tacked.

GOTTFRIED BENN (1886–1956)

Little Aster

A drowned drayman was hoisted on to the slab.
Someone had jammed a lavender aster
between his teeth.
As I made the incision up from the chest
with a long knife
under the skin
to cut out tongue and gums,
I must have nudged it because it slipped
into the brain lying adjacent.
I packed it into the thoracic cavity
with the excelsior
when he was sewn up.
Drink your fill in your vase!
Rest easy,
little aster!

COLEMAN BARKS (b. 1937)

from Body Poems

BRAIN

a flashlight
looking through the empty
limbs

SHOULDER BLADES

the common scallop
shell   broken in two
at its hinge

moves mystically
like it wasn't
hurt

ACHILLES TENDON

walk on your heels
across a puddle:

you mythological
beast

GENITALS

the loaded question:

the slick answer

SKULL

a folk remedy
for the lovesick:

share a meal
of turtle meat

then tack the shell up
for a birdhouse

SCAR

the one chance
I will ever have
to go to Finland

is a long lake
frozen to my leg

Lee Slonimsky (b. 1952)

Schema

"Trees are the veins of the earth,"
you told me,
"carrying an unnameable elixir
from the fire below to the winds above."

Indeed once I glanced in your
surgeon's notebook and saw
a schema just like the convoluted
frame of a tree.

Now I watch the shadows of branches
dancing on this pale March morning
and recall the wonder of your touch
which could set fire to my blood,
make it rush with a roar like wind.

I sigh and the veins outside my window
throb as if they too are moved
by a flow of elixir passing
from earth through trees to sky.

Made in the image of twigs,
my fingertips tremble with loss.

SARAH N. CROSS (b. 1977)

Dear Sir

With my chisel I removed the petrous
portion of your temporal bone to discover
the tiny, majestic malleus attached
to the tympanic membrane—its hanging
no less or more marvelous than vibration.
These are the deepest parts.
I cut the heart from your chest, opened
the thunderous wall of the left ventricle
to touch the billows of the aortic valve—
three smooth leaves, a pale blooming parachute.

So, we have been intimate,
But I do not know you, only imagine
the work you once did in the world
as I peel the sinewy skin
from your palm, its soft pads
finally giving way. I grasp each
finger—from smallest to thumb—
as I loose and then take the muscles
of fine motion which you may have used
to hold those that you loved.

II.

Contagions, Infections, & Fever

WILLIAM BLAKE (1757–1827)

The Sick Rose

O Rose thou art sick.
The invisible worm,
That flies in the night
In the howling storm:

Has found out thy bed
Of crimson joy:
And his dark secret love
Does thy life destroy.

LOUIS SIMPSON (1923–2012)

Typhus

"The whole earth was covered with snow,
and the Snow Queen's sleigh came gliding.
I heard the bells behind me,
and ran, and ran, till I was out of breath."

During the typhus epidemic
she almost died, and would have
but for the woman who lived next door
who cooked for her and watched by the bed.

When she came back to life
and saw herself in a mirror
they had cut off all her hair.
Also, they had burned her clothing,
and her doll, the only one she ever had,
made out of rags and a stick.

Afterwards, they sent her away
to Odessa, to stay with relatives.
The day she was leaving for home
she bought some plums, as a gift
to take back to the family.
They had never seen such plums!
They were in a window, in a basket.
To buy them she spent her last few kopecks.

The journey took three days by train.
It was hot, and the plums were beginning to spoil.
So she ate them . . .
until, finally, all were gone.
The people on the train were astonished.
A child who would eat a plum
and cry . . . then eat another!

*

Her sister, Lisa, died of typhus.
The corpse was laid on the floor.

They carried it to the cemetery
in a box, and brought back the box.
"We were poor—a box was worth something."

LADY MARY WORTLEY MONTAGU (1689–1762)

The Small-Pox

The wretched Flavia on her couch reclin'd,
Thus breath'd the anguish of a wounded mind;
A glass revers'd in her right hand she bore,
For now she shun'd the face she sought before. . . .

'For me the Patriot has the house forsook,
'And left debates to catch a passing look :
'For me the Soldier has soft verses writ;
'For me the Beau has aim'd to be a Wit.
'For me the Wit to nonsense was betray'd;
'The Gamester has for me his dun delay'd,
'And overseen the card, I would have *play'd*.
'The bold and haughty by success made vain,
'Aw'd by my eyes has trembled to complain:
'The bashful 'squire touch'd *by* a wish unknown,
'Has dar'd to speak with spirit not his own;
'Fir'd by one wish, all did alike adore;
'Now beauty's fled, and lovers are no more!

'As round the room I turn my weeping eyes,
'New unaffected scenes of sorrow rise !
'Far from my sight that killing picture bear,
'The face disfigure, *and* the canvas tear !
'That picture which with pride I us'd to show,
'The lost resemblance but upbraids me now.
'And thou, my toilette! where I oft have *sat*,
'While hours unheeded pass'd in deep debate,
'How curls should fall, or where a patch to place :
'If blue or scarlet best became my face;
'Now on some happier nymph thy aid bestow;
'On fairer heads, ye useless jewels glow !
'No borrow'd lustre can my charms restore;
'Beauty is fled, and dress is now no more !

'Ye meaner beauties, I permit *ye* shine;
'Go, triumph in the hearts that once were mine;
'But midst your triumphs with confusion know,
"'Tis to my ruin all your *arms* ye owe.
'Would pitying Heav'n restore my wonted mien,
'*Ye* still might move unthought-of and unseen.
'But oh ! how vain, how wretched is the boast
'Of beauty faded, and of empire lost !
'What now is left but weeping, to deplore
'My beauty fled, and empire now no more! . . . .

OGDEN NASH (1902–1971)

The Common Cold

Go hang yourself, you old M.D.!
You shall no longer sneer at me.
Pick up your hat and stethoscope,
Go wash your mouth with laundry soap;
I contemplate a joy exquisite
In never paying you for your visit.
I did not call you to be told
My malady is a common cold.

By pounding brow and swollen lip;
By fever's hot and scaly grip;
By those two red redundant eyes
That weep like woeful April skies;
By racking snuffle, snort, and sniff;
By handkerchief after handkerchief;
This cold you wave away as naught
Is the damnedest cold man ever caught.

Give ear, you scientific fossil!
Here is the genuine Cold Colossal;
The Cold of which researchers dream,
The Perfect Cold, the Cold Supreme.
This honored system humbly holds
The Super-cold to end all colds;
The Cold Crusading for Democracy;
The Führer of the Streptococcracy.

Bacilli swarm within my portals
Such as were ne'er conceived by mortals,
But bred by scientists wise and hoary
In some Olympic laboratory;
Bacteria as large as mice,
With feet of fire and heads of ice
Who never interrupt for slumber
Their stamping elephantine rumba.

A common cold, forsooth, gadzooks!
Ah, yes. And Lincoln was jostled by Booth;
Don Juan was a budding gallant,
And Shakespeare's plays show signs of talent;
The Arctic winter is fairly coolish,
And your diagnosis is fairly foolish.
Oh what a derision history holds
For the man who belittled the Cold of Colds!

Thom Gunn (1929–2004)

The Man With Night Sweats

I wake up cold, I who
Prospered through dreams of heat
Wake to their residue,
Sweat, and a clinging sheet.

My flesh was its own shield:
Where it was gashed, it healed.

I grew as I explored
The body I could trust
Even while I adored
The risk that made robust,

A world of wonders in
Each challenge to the skin.

I cannot but be sorry
The given shield was cracked,
My mind reduced to hurry,
My flesh reduced and wrecked.

I have to change the bed,
But catch myself instead

Stopped upright where I am
Hugging my body to me
As if to shield it from
The pains that will go through me,

As if hands were enough
To hold an avalanche off.

TED HUGHES (1930–1998)

Fever

You had a fever. You had a real ailment.
You had eaten a baddie.
You lay helpless and a little bit crazy
With the fever. You cried for America
And its medicine cupboard. You tossed
On the immovable Spanish galleon of a bed
In the shuttered Spanish house
That the sunstruck outside glare peered into
As into a tomb. 'Help me,' you whispered, 'help me.'

You rambled. You dreamed you were clambering
Into the well-hatch and, waking, you wanted
To clamber into the well-hatch—the all-clear
Short cut to the cool of the water,
The cool of the dark shaft, the best place
To find oblivion from your burning tangle
And the foreign bug. You cried for certain
You were going to die.
                              I bustled about.
I was nursemaid. I fancied myself at that.
I liked the crisis of the vital role.
I felt things had become real. Suddenly mother,
As a familiar voice, woke in me.
She arrived with certain knowledge. I made a huge soup.
Carrots, tomatoes, peppers and onions,
A rainbow stir of steaming elixir. You
Had to become a sluice, a conduit
Of pure vitamin C. I promised you,
This had saved Voltaire from the plague.
I had to saturate you and flush you
With this simmer of essences.
                              I spooned it
Into your helpless, baby-bird gape, gently,
Masterfully, patiently, hour by hour,
I wiped your tear-ruined face, your exhausted face,

All loose with woe and abandon.
I spooned more and you gulped it like life,
Sobbing, 'I'm going to die.'
                              As I paused
Between your mouthfuls, I stared at the readings
On your dials. Your cry jammed so hard
Over into the red of catastrophe
Left no space for worse. And I thought
How sick is she? Is she exaggerating?
And I recoiled, just a little,
Just for balance, just for symmetry,
Into sceptical patience, a little.
If it can be borne, why make so much of it?
'Come on, now,' I soothed. 'Don't be so scared.
It's only a bug, don't let it run away with you.'

What I was really saying was: 'Stop crying wolf.'
Other thoughts, chilly, familiar thoughts,
Came across the tightrope: 'Stop crying wolf,
Or else I shall not know, I shall not hear
When things get really bad.'
                              It seemed easy
Watching such thoughts come up in such good time.
Plenty of time to think: 'She is crying
As if the most impossible of all
Horrible things had happened—
Had already happened, was going on
Still happening, with the whole world
Too late to help.' Then the blank thought
Of the anaesthesia that helps creatures
Under the polar ice and the callous
That eases overwhelmed doctors. A twisting thought
Of the overload of dilemma, the white-out,
That brings baffled planarian worms to a standstill
Where they curl up and die.

You were overloaded. I said nothing.
I said nothing. The stone man made soup.
The burning woman drank it.

EAVAN BOLAND (b. 1944)

Quarantine

In the worst hour of the worst season
   of the worst year of a whole people
a man set out from the workhouse with his wife.
He was walking—they were both walking—north.

She was sick with famine fever and could not keep up.
   He lifted her and put her on his back.
He walked like that west and west and north.
Until at nightfall under freezing stars they arrived.

In the morning they were both found dead.
   Of cold. Of hunger. Of the toxins of a whole history.
But her feet were held against his breastbone.
The last heat of his flesh was his last gift to her.

Let no love poem ever come to this threshold.
   There is no place here for the inexact
praise of the easy graces and sensuality of the body.
There is only time for this merciless inventory:

Their death together in the winter of 1847.
   Also what they suffered. How they lived.
And what there is between a man and a woman.
And in which darkness it can best be proved.

Thomas James (1946–1974)

In Fever

The field is white at the beginning
Of October. The crows are emptying their cries
Into the blank memory of heaven.

The front porch is cool all morning.
I watch the thistles moving their shabby weapons
Like a field of bad dreams.

The geranium pots are spilled
Over the flagstones.
There are splinters in the dry stalks.

The cry of a door is a pitiable thing.
Love, I am useless as a burnt-out match—
Your hands have sponged my body twice a day,

I am fed on stale water
And a light mixed in the center of the mirror,
The bottom of an ancient woman's cauldron.

The bedsprings are crying.
I move into sleep, climbing ten crumbling steps
Into a tawdry mansion.

CLARINDA HARRISS (b. 1939)

U.S. Marine with AIDS

poses in full dress for *The Morning Sun*,
purple heart on his shrunken chest.
Lies propped on a hospital cot
somewhere in coalmine territory. Blond
goatteed, mustachioed, thin as any
POW but most like a Union soldier:
blue-high-collared, brass buttoned,
formal, bristling with rectitude,
dead, it would seem, except for
wide defiant eyes. Huge toddlers
line up with the anxious wife
on either side of where he lies.
He has shrunk smaller than life.

Make my bed narrow, make my bed soon

A hundred years ago they shot family
photographs with one dead member—
some, sometimes, in uniform—
propped stiff among the living.
And exquisite tintypes of dead
babies in christening gowns

for my heart's blood's aspilling
and I fain would lie down.

By sunny noon on Monument Street
half a dozen of the troops
Captain Hooker lent his name to
start marching their brassy uniforms
up and down the downtown curb
saluting Acuras and Saabs:
"Want to party? Want a date?"
One big brownstone house preserves
the Maryland Historical Society

where the dress suits soldiers wore
in 1812 and 1865 rot quietly
on mannequins' wire shoulders—
seeming too small for a grown man
but just right, soon, for a few
shrinking boys with traitor blood,
boys dying for their photographs
to be propped on some sad mantel.

Mother, mother, make my bed,
make it soft and narrow;
since my love died for me today
I'll die for him tomorrow.

Bob Hicok (b. 1960)

Extreme Measures

Blood was once thought a cure for epilepsy
and some Romans,
possessed by the disorder,
sucked the wounds of defeated gladiators.
Picture a Senator, vampire by prescription,
leaning over a dying man,
drinking the remedy for the storms
which throw his body down,
straighten his spine, shoot out his tongue
and often leave no memory of the event,
slicing away tiny portions of his life.
Blood's now asylum for a virus
scrawnier than a wavelength of visible light,
an indiscriminate parasite
which views the needled
and pimped
and loved
alike.
Desperate, some with AIDS
pop nerve-wasting drugs,
drink urine, shock flesh,
arrange blood stones under their beds
in patterns shamans would envy,
down extracts of marrow and cucumber,
potions promising a wonder fix,
the red cheeks and high fives
of good heath. In extremis
the extreme appeals, offers the carnival ride
of another chance,
and until the immunological tumblers click
and champagne's popped in some lab,
there'll be a legion of gaunt believers
in the voodoo of the long shot,
their lives reduced
to the death-row philosophy

of nothing to lose.
Spes, the Roman goddess of hope,
holds a bud
that blooms to the light of her patient eyes.
Were we in the business of making gods today,
our Hope would be a hunter,
lean as fear
with bright and savage eyes.

STEPHEN DUNN (b. 1939)

Plaisir

Diarrhea: what nobody likes,
though a word the French love to pronounce.
They surround it with lips and tongue
it pleases, like saying *cellar door* does.
Once I gave a pair of tweezers
to an *au pair* girl who couldn't extract
a splinter from her foot. It was a pleasure
for both of us to see that little thing come out.

JASON SHINDER (1955–2008)

How I Am

When I talk to my friends I pretend I am standing on the wing

of a flying plane. I cannot be trusted to tell them how I am.
Or if I am falling to earth weighing less

than a dozen roses. Sometimes I dream they have broken up

with their lovers and are carrying food to my house.
When I open the mailbox I hear their voices

like the long upwardwinding curve of a train whistle

passing through the tall grasses and ferns
after the train has passed. I never get ahead of their shadows;

I embrace them in front of moving cars.

I keep them away from my misery
because to say I am miserable is to say I am like them.

CLAUDIA EMERSON (1957–2014)

The Polio Vaccine, Chatman, Virginia, 1964

for Inez Shields

It was not death we came to fear but her life,
her other birth, waking remade from the womb

of that disease. One leg was withered, a dragging-
numb weight behind her, one shoulder humped—

a camel's—and what did we know of that foreign
beast but ugliness and that she carried in it hard

faith like water. And so we did what we were told:
outside the elementary school, the long line drowsed.

We saw gleaming trays of sugar cubes rose-pink
with the livid virus tamed, its own undoing.

We opened our mouths, held it on our tongues
and, as with any candy, savored the sharp corners

going, the edges, until at last the form gave way
to grain, to sweet sand washing against the salt of us.

Ogden Nash (1902–1971)

The Germ

A mighty creature is the germ,
Though smaller than the pachyderm.
His customary dwelling place
Is deep within the human race.
His childish pride he often pleases
By giving people strange diseases.
Do you, dear reader, feel infirm?
You probably contain a germ.

STANLEY PLUMLY (b. 1939)

The Iron Lung

So this is the dust that passes through porcelain,
so this is the unwashed glass left over from supper,
so this is the air in the attic, in August,
and this the down on the breath of the sleeper . . .

If we could fold our arms, but we can't.
If we could cross our legs, but we can't.
If we could put the mind to rest . . .
But our fathers have set this task before us.

My face moons in the mirror, weightless,
without air, my head propped like a penny.
I'm dressed in a shoe, ready to walk out
of here. I'm wearing my father's body.

I remember my mother standing in the doorway
trying to tell me something. The day is thick
with the heat rising from the road. I am
too far away. She looks like my sister.

And I am dreaming of my mother in a doorway
telling my father to die or go away.
It is the front door, and my drunken father falls
to the porch on his knees like one of his children.

It is precisely at this moment I realize
I have polio and will never walk again.
And I am in the road on my knees, like my father,
but as if I were growing into the ground

I can neither move nor rise.
The neighborhood is gathering, and now
my father is lifting me into the ambulance
among the faces of my family. His face is

a blur or a bruise and he holds me
as if I had just been born. When I wake
I am breathing out of all proportion to myself.
My whole body is a lung; I am floating

above a doorway or grave. And I know
I am in this breathing room as one
who understands how breath is passed
from father to son and passed back again.

At night, when my father comes to talk,
I tell him we have shared this body long enough.
He nods, like the speaker in a dream.
He knows that I know we're only talking.

Once there was a machine for breathing.
It would embrace the body and make a kind of love.
And when it was finished it would rise
like nothing at all above the earth

to drift through the daylight silence.
But at dark, in deep summer, if you thought you heard
something like your mother's voice calling you home,
you could lie down where you were and listen to the dead

C. DALE YOUNG (b. 1969)

Sepsis

The fog has yet to lift, God, and still the bustle
of buses and garbage trucks. God, I have coveted
sleep. I have wished to find an empty bed
in the hospital while on call. I have placed
my bodily needs first, left nurses to do
what I should have done. And so, the antibiotics
sat on the counter. They sat on the counter
under incandescent lights. No needle was placed
in the woman's arm. No IV was started. It sat there
on the counter waiting. I have coveted sleep, God,
and the toxins I studied in Bacteriology took hold
of Your servant. When the blood flowered
beneath her skin, I shocked her, placed the paddles
on her chest, her dying body convulsing each time.
The antibiotics sat on the counter, and shame
colored my face, the blood pooling in my cheeks
like heat. And outside, the stars continued falling
into place. And the owl kept talking without listening.
And the wind kept sweeping the streets clean.
And the heart in my chest stayed silent.
How could I have known that I would never forget,
that early some mornings, in the waking time,
the fog still filling the avenues, that the image
of her body clothed in sweat would find me?
I have disobeyed my Oath. I have caused harm.
I have failed the preacher from the Baptist Church.
Dear God, how does a sinner outlast the sin?

III.

Blindness, Pain, & Other Ailments

Rainer Maria Rilke (1875–1926)

Going Blind

She sat just like the others at the table.
But on second glance, she seemed to hold her cup
a little differently as she picked it up.
She smiled once. It was almost painful.

And when they finished and it was time to stand
and slowly, as chance selected them, they left
and moved through many rooms (they talked and laughed),
I saw her. She was moving far behind

the others, absorbed, like someone who will soon
have to sing before a large assembly;
upon her eyes, which were radiant with joy,
light played as on the surface of a pool.

She followed slowly, taking a long time,
as though there were some obstacle in the way;
and yet: as though, once it was overcome,
she would be beyond all walking, and would fly.

CLAUDIA EMERSON (1957–2014)

Migraine: Aura and Aftermath

First, part of the world disappears. Something
is missing from everything: the cat's eye,
ear, the left side of its face; two fingers
from my right hand; the words from the end
of a sentence. The absence is at first
more absolute than whatever darkness
I imagine the blind perceive. Perfect,
without color or motion, nothing replaces

what is gone. The senses do not contradict. My arm
goes numb, my leg. Though I have felt the cold air
of this disappearance before, each time the aura
deceives me to believe reality itself
has failed. I fear this more than what it warns
because I cannot remember I will survive it.

The other half of me will shine all night,
defined by the eclipse.
                        Then, in the relieved
wake of the day that follows it, I will
find my hand, count my fingers, and beginning
to see again, will recognize myself
restored to the evening of a righted room.

Emily Dickinson (1830–1886)

Pain has an Element of Blank

Pain—has an Element of Blank—
It cannot recollect
When it begun—or if there were
A time when it was not—

It has no Future—but itself—
Its Infinite contain
Its Past—enlightened to perceive
New Periods—of Pain.

YEHUDA AMICHAI (1924–2000)

When I Have a Stomachache

When I have stomachache, I feel like
the whole round globe.
When I have a headache, laughter
bursts out in the wrong place in my body.
And when I cry, they're putting my father in the ground
in a grave that's too big for him, and he won't
grow to fit it.
And if I'm a hedgehog, I'm a hedgehog in reverse,
the spikes grow inward and stab.
And if I'm the prophet Ezekiel, I see
in the Vision of the Chariot
only the dung-spattered feet of oxen and the muddy wheels.

I'm like a porter carrying a heavy armchair
on his back to some faraway place
without knowing he can put it down and sit in it.

I'm like a rifle that's a little out of date
but very accurate: when I love,
there's a strong recoil, back to childhood, and it hurts.

SIR ARTHUR CONAN DOYLE (1859–1930)

Religio Medici

God's own best will bide the test
    And God's own worst will fall;
But, best or worst or last or first,
    He ordereth it all.

For *all* is good, if understood,
    (Ah, could we understand!)
And right and ill are tools of skill
    Held in His either hand.

The harlot and the anchorite,
    The martyr and the rake,
Deftly He fashions each aright,
    Its vital part to take.

Wisdom He makes to form the fruit
    Where the high blossoms be;
And Lust to kill the weaker shoot,
    And Drink to trim the tree.

And Holiness that so the bole
    Be solid at the core;
And Plague and Fever, that the whole
    Be changing evermore.

He strews the microbes in the lung,
    The blood-clot in the brain;
With test and test He picks the best,
    Then tests them once again.

He tests the body and the mind,
    He rings them o'er and o'er;
And if they crack, He throws them back,
    And fashions them once more.

He chokes the infant throat with slime,
    He sets the ferment free;
He builds the tiny tube of lime
    That blocks the artery.

He lets the youthful dreamer store
    Great projects in his brain,
Until He drops the fungus spore
    That smears them out again.

He stores the milk that feeds the babe,
    He dulls the tortured nerve;
He gives a hundred joys of sense
    Where few or none might serve.

And still He trains the branch of good
    Where the high blossoms be,
And wieldeth still the shears of ill
    To prune and prune His tree.

B. H. FAIRCHILD (b. 1942)

Flight

*"In the early stages of epilepsy there occurs a characteristic dream.
One is somehow lifted free of one's own body; looking back one
sees oneself and feels a sudden, maddening fear; another presence
is entering one's own person, and there is no avenue of return."*
—George Steiner

Outside my window the wasps
are making their slow circle,
dizzy flights of forage and return,
hovering among azaleas
that bob in a sluggish breeze
this humid, sun-torn morning.

Yesterday my wife held me here
as I thrashed and moaned, her hand
in my foaming mouth, and my son
saw what he was warned he might.

Last night dreams stormed my brain
in thick swirls of shame and fear.
Behind a white garage a locked shed
full of wide-eyed dolls burned,
yellow smoke boiling up in huge clumps
as I watched, feet nailed to the ground.
In dining cars white table cloths
unfolded wings and flew like gulls.
An old German in a green Homburg
sang lieder, *Mein Herz ist müde.*
In a garden in Pasadena my father
posed in Navy whites while overhead
silver dirigibles moved like great whales.
And in the narrowing tunnel
of the dream's end I flew down
onto the iron red road
of my grandfather's farm.

There was a white rail fence.
In the green meadow beyond,
a small boy walked toward me.
His smile was the moon's rim.
Across his egg-shell eyes
ran scenes from my future life,
and he embraced me like a son
or father or my lost brother.

FLOYD SKLOOT (b. 1947)

The Onset of Vertigo

I woke one morning to a whirling world.
The room spun counterclockwise, taking me
down with it. On all fours, I watched
the door jamb sway and thought *earthquake*.
But the floor was still and the walls held
together. So this was going on inside
my head. I spoke to see if I could,
blinked to see if that changed the way
I saw things, moved fingers and toes,
rocked back on my naked haunches.
My head didn't hurt. I knew where I was
in the world and time. My wife stirred
behind me in bed. I tried to calm myself:
over sixty, rose too quickly, wax in ears,
sudden change of weather in the early
spring. A dream. Nothing to worry about.
Nothing to say it would last six months.
I would stand if I could get a grip on
something more solid than undulating air.

KAY RYAN (b. 1945)

Tired Blood

Well, not *tired*
so much as *freighted.*
As though foreign objects
had invaded.
As though tiny offices
had dumped
their metal furniture
among the glossy lozenges
and platelets—
chairs that stick together,
painful cabinets.

SHARON DOLIN (b. 1956)

Stroke

These days being so fuzzy-headed I go
into the Greek diner on 72nd Street the scaffolding

up all winter finally gone so the late spring light
streams through & I sit in the corner booth & order the usual

dark-meat turkey on rye which is almost a poem & a soda
when she limps in with one metal arm brace says hi to everyone

& me sits down at the next booth on the other side
two men are striking a deal about something in film

only her left arm works so it takes a while to slip everything
off & slide into the seat with her big belly a silver caduceus

flopping over her breasts she says hi to me a second time I'm watching
her closely since we share a not-so-secret sisterhood of the belly

though I'm a fairly new member I get up the nerve to ask
how many months & she struggles gesturing blurts I've-Had-a-Stroke

writes 6 over and over on the Formica with her left forefinger
until I nod then point to my belly hold up 4 fingers Nice-Beautiful

& we go on talking in gestures & simple retorts Makes-Sense-
Yes the waitress holds the menu up so she must be a regular

here & writes out TOAST so she can nod then tells me
IVF . . . Once-Nothing-Twice-Nothing-By-Myself-Beautiful

then points to me IVF-Once-Nothing-By-Myself-Chinese-Herbs
& she Yes! Makes-Sense! How old is she—38. How old am I—41.

Nice-Great-Makes-Sense-So-Worried when I ask about the stroke
she holds up 7 fingers for years. Have you tried . . . Everything she

waves it all away points to my small belly—Beautiful—now it's almost
    time
to go what can I give her I hold open a gallery catalogue bright swanks
    of color

You? No I write POET—Understand—She? After-No-Before Invest . . .
    Investment
Banker? Yes—Her name? Broo-Broomah . . . can't say it when the
    waitress returns

says Bluma And Yours? Sharon Nice-Makes-Sense

FREDERICK SEIDEL (b. 1936)

Dune Road, Southhampton

The murderer has been injecting her remorselessly
With succinylcholine, which he mixes in her daily insulin.
She's too weak to give herself her shots. By the time she has figured it out,
She is helpless.

She can't move any part of her face.
She can't write a note.
She can't speak
To say she hasn't had a stroke.

It's terrifying that she's aware
That something terrible is being done to her.
One day he ups the dose. And gets scared.
She has to be rushed to the local hospital and intubated.

They know at the hospital who she is,
One of the richest women in the world.
The murderer hands the attending a faked M.R.I.
It flaunts the name of a world authority. Showing she has had a stroke.

The neurologist on call introduces herself to the murderer and concurs.
Locked-in syndrome, just about the worst.
Alive, with staring eyes.
The mind is unaffected.

And with the patient looking on expressionlessly,
Screaming don't let him take me home, without a sign or sound,
The doctor tells the murderer he can take her home,
If that's their wish.

Their little beach house has forty rooms.
Her elevator is carved mahogany.
The Great Gatsby swimming pool upstairs is kept full and never used.
Her tower bedroom flies out over the winter ocean, spreading its wings.

Mother, you're going to die,
He tells her, once they're alone.
You have the right to remain silent.
I'm making a joke.

WILLIAM EMPSON (1906–1984)

Missing Dates

Slowly the poison the whole blood stream fills.
It is not the effort nor the failure tires.
The waste remains, the waste remains and kills.

It is not your system or clear sight that mills
Down small to the consequence a life requires;
Slowly the poison the whole blood stream fills.

They bled an old dog dry yet the exchange rills
Of young dog blood gave but a month's desires;
The waste remains, the waste remains and kills.

It is the Chinese tombs and the slag hills
Usurp the soil, and not the soil retires.
Slowly the poison the whole blood stream fills.

Not to have fire is to be a skin that shrills.
The complete fire is death. From partial fires
The waste remains, the waste remains and kills.

It is the poems you have lost, the ills
From missing dates, at which the heart expires.
Slowly the poison the whole blood stream fills.
The waste remains, the waste remains and kills.

BRIAN THORNTON (b. 1975)

Losing -*lar degener*-

*Macular Degeneration—the progressive deterioration of a critical region
of the retina called the macula. The macula is a 3–5 mm area in the retina
that is responsible for central vision. This disorder leads to irreversible loss
of central vision, although peripheral vision is retained but may be gray,
hazy, or distorted.*

You hide

behind vascular walls   in veils of Vaseline
pinpricking tiny tiles   beneath coated corneas
misunderstood macu   ation reflection smearing
Doctors become Bob and Jill   peeling envy
with scalpels and suction cups   from faces lost
with promises of promises   as memory fades
from fractal foreign lands   quenching the distance
of scientific breakthroughs   in forgetfulness
of protein inhibitors   Eventually
Promises of sight become   a false supposition
a faith   of non-existence

You lose

tile after tile dot after dot   your eyes
confined to feel light with   your lips
a new sense of   your color
You feel ugly   You are beautiful
There is a rotten stench   in absence
like electrical fire   to the curious mind
charring neural receptors   feeding blank pages
as each destined tile falls   teasing with tiny flashes
susceptible to losing face   yet privy to hushed whispers
behind the next white curtain   where letters play

childish games

John Milton (1608–1674)

On His Blindness

When I consider how my light is spent
Ere half my days in this dark world and wide
And that one talent which is death to hide
Lodged with me useless, though my soul more bent
To serve therewith my Maker, and present
My true account, lest he returning chide,
"Doth God exact day labor, light denied?"
I fondly ask. But Patience, to prevent
That murmur, soon replies,."God doth not need
Either man's work or his own gifts. Who best
Bear his mild yoke, they serve him best. His state
Is kingly: thousands at his bidding speed
And post o'er land and ocean without rest:
They also serve who only stand and wait."

Thomas James (1946–1974)

Snakebite

Now I am getting light as cotton candy—
Out of the two red holes in my heel
Infinity pours, goodbye to all of me.
It was pleasant to watch my leg begin to swell;
An incredible headiness washed over me,
I didn't feel a thing. The color of a bluebottle,

The sky hit my skin like water from a pitcher.
I remember only a limber brown stick
Without any fangs, then the cool white stretcher
Where I became part of an unamusing joke
And the sun became a singular gold adder,
Which gathered its constricted shape and struck.

First I dream of wool, and then of water,
The bridge gone out under my footsoles.
Sleep eddies under everything pure as a colt's star.
These ladies in white speak of a mouthful of bells.
They let the sleep rush out of me like air
Out of an innertube, smudging their white walls.

Watching milady through the wrong end of the telescope,
I suck the glass pencil at noonday.
Here is a pale horse, they say; this is his stirrup.
I ride on my own diminishing. I grow gray
In the mild contagion of my sleep.
The light spreads its thin skin and grows muddy.

They feed me through tubes and comfort me with needles.
Where are the nubile, white-winged ladies
Who populate these immaculate halls?
The young men who view me have sulphur-blue jaws
They do not complain. They bring me bottles
Of adamant, they move quietly as butterflies

And are upon me when I least expect it.
Everything I leave behind is ubiquitous,
Even the undependable broad daylight
Which grows thinner each time I raise my eyes
To watch the centuries stream from my foot
And the whole world rock backward into place.

IV.

POWDERS, PILLS, & OTHER REMEDIES

OVID (43 B.C.–A.D. 17)

from The Art of Beauty

Although incense is pleasing to the gods and soothes their wrath, it must not be kept exclusively for their altars. A mixture of incense and nitre is good for black-heads. Take four ounces of each. Add an ounce of gum from the bark of a tree, and a little cube of oily myrrh. Crush the whole together and pass through a sieve. Bind the resultant powder by mixing with honey. Some people recommend that fennel should be added to the myrrh; nine scruples of myrrh and five of fennel is the proportion. Add a handful of dried rose-leaves, some sal-ammoniac and male frankincense. Pour on barley-water, and let the weight of the sal-ammoniac and the incense equal the weight of the roses. After employing very few applications of this mixture, you will have a charming complexion.

GOTTFRIED BENN (1886–1956)

Zeh Was a Pharmacist

Zeh was a pharmacist,
or claimed to be,
times were tranquil, people didn't ask too many questions,
but when a new broom came along, it was duly
     "established that" etc.
and it all contributed to his downfall.

Zeh was an incomparable magician
shelves full of powders and tinctures
not that he had to sell them to you
you were persuaded of their efficacy
in advance.

Zeh had mixed up a slimming-cure
called Zeean that you hardly even needed to take
it worked in your pocket
you straightaway started to reduce.
He had stuck that preparation
     in one of the pharmacy windows.

Among other things you could see there
herbal teas, pestles and mortars, chatty tips
for di- and nocturnal events of an untoward nature
all of it defying description—
unrivaled in their suggestiveness
from a psychosomatic point of view

his like would never be found again
children (not likely!) *desunt*,
long since turfed out of his grave.

AMY CLAMPITT (1920–1994)

A Cure at Porlock

For whatever did it—the cider
at the Ship Inn, where the crowd
from the bar that night had overflowed
singing into Southey's Corner, or

an early warning of appendicitis—
the remedy the chemist in the High Street
purveyed was still a dose of kaopectate
in morphine—the bane and the afflatus

of S.T.C. when Alph, the sacred river,
surfaced briefly in the unlikely
vicinity of Baker Farm, and as quickly
sank again, routed forever by the visitor

whose business, intent and disposition—
whether ill or well is just as immaterial—
long ago sunk Lethewards, a particle
of the unbottled ultimate solution.

I drank my dose, and after an afternoon
prostrate, between heaves, on the
coldly purgatorial tiles of the W.C.,
found it elysium simply to recline,

sipping flat ginger beer as though it were
honeydew, in that billowy bed,
under pink chenille, hearing you read
The Mystery of Edwin Drood! For whether

the opium was worth it for John Jasper,
from finding being with you, even sick
at Porlock, a rosily addictive picnic,
I left less likely ever to recover.

A Receipt to Cure the Vapours

I

Why will Delia thus retire,
    And idly languish life away?
While the sighing crowd admire,
    'Tis too soon for hartshorn tea.

II

All those dismal looks and fretting
    Cannot Damon's life restore:
Long ago the worms have eat him,
    You can never see him more.

III

Once again consult your toilette,
    In the glass your face review:
So much weeping soon will spoil it,
    And no spring your charms renew.

IV

I, like you, was born a woman,
    Well I know what vapours mean:
The disease, alas! is common;
    Single, we have all the spleen.

V

All the morals that they tell us,
    Never cur'd the sorrow yet:
Chuse, among the pretty fellows,
    One of honour, youth, and wit.

VI

Prithee hear him ev'ry morning,
    At the least an hour or two;
Once again at night returning—
    I believe the dose will do.

ANNA SEWARD (1742–1809)

Sonnet: To the Poppy

While Summer roses all their glory yield
   To crown the votary of love and joy,
   Misfortune's victim hails, with many a sigh,
   Thee, scarlet Poppy of the pathless field,
Gaudy, yet wild and lone; no leaf to shield
   Thy flaccid vest, that, as the gale blows high,
   Flaps, and alternate folds around thy head.—
   So stands in the long grass a love-craz'd maid,
Smiling aghast; while stream to every wind
   Her garish ribbons, smear'd with dust and rain;
   But brain-sick visions cheat her tortur'd mind,
And bring false peace. Thus, lulling grief and pain,
   Kind dreams oblivious from thy juice proceed,
   Thou flimsy, showy, melancholy Weed.

HENRY DAVID THOREAU (1817–1862)

To a Marsh Hawk in Spring

There is health in thy gray wing
Health of nature's furnishing.
Say thou modern-winged antique,
Was thy mistress ever sick?
In each heaving of thy wing
Thou dost health and leisure bring,
Thou dost waive disease & pain
And resume new life again.

PHILIP LARKIN (1922–1985)

Faith Healing

Slowly the women file to where he stands
Upright in rimless glasses, silver hair,
Dark suit, white collar. Stewards tirelessly
Persuade them onwards to his voice and hands,
Within whose warm spring rain of loving care
Each dwells some twenty seconds. *Now, dear child,
What's wrong*, the deep American voice demands,
And, scarcely pausing, goes into a prayer
Directing God about this eye, that knee.
Their heads are clasped abruptly; then, exiled

Like losing thoughts, they go in silence; some
Sheepishly stray, not back into their lives
Just yet; but some stay stiff, twitching and loud
With deep hoarse tears, as if a kind of dumb
And idiot child within them still survives
To re-awake at kindness, thinking a voice
At last calls them alone, that hands have come
To lift and lighten; and such joy arrives
Their thick tongues blort, their eyes squeeze grief, a crowd
Of huge unheard answers jam and rejoice—

What's wrong! Moustached in flowered frocks they shake:
By now, all's wrong. In everyone there sleeps
A sense of life lived according to love.
To some it means the difference they could make
By loving others, but across most it sweeps
As all they might have done had they been loved.
That nothing cures. An immense slackening ache,
As when, thawing, the rigid landscape weeps,
Spreads slowly through them—that, and the voice above
Saying *Dear child*, and all time has disproved.

ALICE FULTON (b. 1952)

Claustrophilia

It's just me throwing myself at you,
romance as usual, us times us,

not lust but moxibustion,
a substance burning close

to the body as possible
without risk of immolation.

Nearness without contact
causes numbness. Analgesia.

Pins and needles. As the snugness
of the surgeon's glove causes hand fatigue.

At least this procedure
requires no swag or goody bags,

stuff bestowed upon the stars
at their luxe functions.

There's no dress code,
though leg irons

are always appropriate.
And if anyone says what the hell

are you wearing in Esperanto—
Kion diable vi portas?—

tell them anguish
is the universal language.

Stars turn to train wrecks
and my heart goes out,

admirers gush. Ground to a velvet!
But never mind the downside,

mon semblable, mon crush.
Love is just the retaliation of light.

It is so profligate, you know,
so rich with rush.

HENRY WADSWORTH LONGFELLOW (1807–1882)

from Hiawatha's Lamentation

. . . . Then the Medicine-men, the Medas,
The magicians, the Wabenos,
And the Jossakeeds, the prophets,
Came to visit Hiawatha;
Built a Sacred Lodge beside him,
To appease him, to console him,
Walked in silent, grave procession,
Bearing each a pouch of healing,
Skin of beaver, lynx, or otter,
Filled with magic roots and simples,
Filled with very potent medicines.

    When he heard their steps approaching,
Hiawatha ceased lamenting,
Called no more on Chibiabos;
Naught he questioned, naught he answered,
But his mournful head uncovered,
From his face the mourning colors
Washed he slowly and in silence,
Slowly and in silence followed
Onward to the Sacred Wigwam.

    There a magic drink they gave him,
Made of Nahma-wusk, the spearmint,
And Wabeno-wusk, the yarrow,
Roots of power, and herbs of healing;
Beat their drums, and shook their rattles;
Chanted singly and in chorus,
Mystic songs like these, they chanted.

    "I myself, myself! behold me!
'Tis the great Gray Eagle talking;
Come, ye white crows, come and hear him!
The loud-speaking thunder helps me;
All the unseen spirits help me;
I can hear their voices calling,
All around the sky I hear them!

I can blow you strong, my brother,
I can heal you, Hiawatha!"

.... Then they shook their medicine-pouches
O'er the head of Hiawatha,
Danced their medicine-dance around him;
And upstarting wild and haggard,
Like a man from dreams awakened,
He was healed of all his madness.
As the clouds are swept from heaven,
Straightway from his brain departed
All his moody melancholy;
As the ice is swept from rivers,
Straightway from his heart departed
All his sorrow and affliction.

.... Forth then issued Hiawatha,
Wandered eastward, wandered westward,
Teaching men the use of simples
And the antidotes for poisons,
And the cure of all diseases.
Thus was first made known to mortals
All the mystery of Medamin,
All the sacred art of healing.

THOMAS LOVELL BEDDOES (1803–1849)

Resurrection Song

Thread the nerves through the right holes,
Get out of my bones, you wormy souls.
Shut up my stomach, the ribs are full:
Muscles be steady and ready to pull.
Heart and artery merrily shake
And eyelid go up, for we're going to wake.—
His eye must be brighter—one more rub!
And pull up the nostrils! his nose was snub.

Miroslav Holub (1923–1998)

from Interferon

Always just one demon in the attic.
Always just one death in the village. And the dogs
howling in that direction. And from the other end
the new-born child arrives, the only one
to fill the empty space in that wide air.

Likewise also cells infected by a virus
send out a signal all around them and defences
are mobilised so that no other virus
has any hope just then of taking root
or changing fate. This phenomenon
is known as interference.

And when a poet dies in the depth of night
a single black bird wakens in the thicket
and sings for all it is worth
while from the sky a black rain trickles down
like sperm or something,
the song is spattered and the choking bird
sings sitting on an empty rib-cage
in which an imaginary heart
awakes to its forever interfering
futility. And in the morning the sky is clear,
the bird is weary and the soil is fertilised.
The poet is no more.

In Klatovy Street, in Pilsen,
by the railway bridge, there was
a shop with quilted bedcovers.
In times when there's a greater need
for a steel cover over our continent
business in quilted bedcovers
is slack. The shopkeeper was hard up.
Practical men when hard up usually
turn to art.

In his shopwindow, open to the interior
of his shop, its owner built
a gingerbread house of quilts
and every evening staged
a performance about a quilted
gingerbread house and a red-quilted
Little Red Riding Hood, while his wife
in this quilted masquerade was alternately
the wolf or the witch, and he himself
a padded-out Hansel,
or Gretel, Red Riding Hood or grandmother.
The sight of the two old people
crawling about in swollen billows
of textiles round the chubby cottage
was not unambiguous. It was a little like
the life of sea cucumbers in the mud
under a reef. Outside thundered
the approaching surf of war and they
conducted their quilted
pantomime outside time and action.

For a while children would stand outside but
soon they would go home. Nothing was sold.
But it was the only pantomime
at that time. The black bird sang
and rain poured into a rib-cage
wearing the Star of David. . . .

The black bird sang and the ruined
sclerotic hearts leapt in their breasts,
and then one morning when they didn't play
and had not even raised the blind—
the sky was clear, the soil was fertilized—
the quilted bedcovers were confiscated
for the eastern front and the actors

transferred to the backstage
of the world, called Bergen-Belsen.
No trace is left of the shop today:
it's now a greengrocer's with woody parsnips. . . .

When we did autopsies at the psychiatric
hospital in Bohnice, filled with the
urban exudations of relative futility,
the car would tip us out amidst the ward blocks
whose inmates waved from windows
with some kind of May Day pennants, and then
one went, hugely alone,
beyond a spinney to the solitary morgue, where
the naked bodies of ancient schizophrenics
awaited us, along with two live inmates; one of them
would pull the corpses up from underground
with a rope hoist and place them
upon the tables as a mother might an infant
for baptism, while the other was lurking, pen ready poised,
in a dark corner to write up
the Latin protocol, and he wrote faultlessly.
Neither of them uttered the slightest sound, only
the hoist shaft moaned . . . and the knife
drawn over skin and dermis made a sound
of satin tearing...and they were always
enormous and unprecedented pneumonias
and tumours big as dragons' eggs,
it rained into the open thorax—
and in that roaring silence one had to
break the line of an angel's fall
and dictate the logical verdict
on a long-sentenced demon . . .
and the schizophrenic's pen in the corner
busily scraped across the paper
like an eager mouse.

We need no prompters
said the puppets haughtily.

The air of that anatomical theatre
was filled with interferon,
it was a great personal demonstration
against malignant growth, it was
a general amnesty for the walls, entropy
was abjured for the moment

because there are no bubbles at the bottom
to burst under the breeze . . .

Once on St Nicholas' Day, the man acting the Devil,
dead drunk, fell down some stairs and lay there,
and a child, experiencing that embarrassing
joy mere inches from terror,
ran out after the thump and called:

Mummy, come here, there's a dead devil—

And so he was, even though the actor
picked himself up after another tot. Maybe the dogs howled,
but only by a black mistake.
In the sky shone the stars of the main sequence,
the bird was getting ready in the thicket,
the child shivered a little
from the chill of three million years,
in that wide air, but
they prompted him, poetically,

you're only imagining all this,
look, the butterfly's already
bringing the flowers back . . . and
there's no other devil left . . . and
the nearer paradise . . .

He believed, and yet he didn't.

WISŁAWA SZYMBORSKA (1923–2012)

Advertisement

I'm a tranquillizer.
I'm effective at home.
I work in the office.
I can take exams
or the witness stand.
I mend broken cups with care.
All you have to do is take me,
let me melt beneath your tongue,
just gulp me
with a glass of water.

I know how to handle misfortune,
how to take bad news.
I can minimize injustice,
lighten up God's absence,
or pick the widow's veil that suits your face.
What are you waiting for—
have faith in my chemical compassion.

You're still a young man/woman.
It's not too late to learn how to unwind.
Who said
you have to take it on the chin?

Let me have your abyss.
I'll cushion it with sleep.
You'll thank me for giving you
four paws to fall on.

Sell me your soul.
There are no other takers.

There is no other devil anymore.

Tom Healy (b. 1961)

Voodoo

Everyone is so involved
keeping track of my pills:

my husband, his secretary,
our protective housekeeper

who counts them out in Creole,
numbering a scattered universe

of nebulae clustered on the bed
when she helps me pack

for Florida or days
an even greater distance

lays claim to. She says
it's like the rosary,

counting and whispering,
and she teaches me words

for purple, white, yellow, a shock
of orange, two different blues,

and a curse on one that's striped
turquoise and kelly green.

KAY RYAN (b. 1945)

Bitter Pill

A bitter pill
doesn't need
to be swallowed
to work. Just
reading your name
on the bottle
does the trick.
As though there
were some anti-
placebo effect.
As though the
self were eager
to be wrecked.

GRACE SCHULMAN (b. 1935)

Query

Is there a healing twig or plume,
a rod or wizard's tea, a spell,
a paste of flowers and their stems
to lift my love and make him whole?

I'd see him take these rocky stairs
two after two, down to a park
that overflows with sycamores
whose twisted limbs have just come back

to sprout, renewed, on paths so thin,
so dense with green, he'd lose his way,
search for an iron bridge or pond,
and know, just as a ball let fly

sails back, he would walk out again.
When science shrugs, where is the stone
that mends, the dung beetle that cures.
Or, surely if some words on fire

can kill, others can right a wrong.
Shaman, teach me a chant to ban
pain. For it, take all my songs,
whose cures, if any, are unknown.

V.

From the Children's Ward

ROBERT LOUIS STEVENSON (1850–1894)

The Sick Child

Child—
O mother, lay your hand on my brow!
O mother, mother, where am I now?
Why is the room so gaunt and great?
Why am I lying awake so late?

Mother—
Fear not at all: the night is still.
Nothing is here that means you ill—
Nothing but lamps the whole town through,
And never a child awake but you.

Child—
Mother, mother, speak low in my ear,
Some of the things are so great and near,
Some are so small and far away,
I have a fear that I cannot say.
What have I done, and what do I fear,
And why are you crying, mother dear?

Mother—
Out in the city, sounds begin
Thank the kind God, the carts come in!
An hour or two more and God is so kind,
The day shall be blue in the windowblind,
Then shall my child go sweetly asleep,
And dream of the birds and the hills of sheep.

ELLEN BRYANT VOIGT (b. 1943)

Damage

It didn't suckle. That
was the first indication.

Looking back, I know how much I knew.
The repetitious bloodfall,

the grating at the door of bone,
the afterbirth stuck in my womb like a scab.

Others were lucky,
response was taken from them.

Each time I bathe him
in his little tub, I think

How easy to let go

Let go

SYLVIA PLATH (1932–1963)

Thalidomide

O half moon—

Half-brain, luminosity—
Negro, masked like a white,

Your dark
Amputations crawl and appall—

Spidery, unsafe.
What glove

What leatheriness
Has protected

Me from that shadow—
The indelible buds,

Knuckles at shoulder-blades, the
Faces that

Shove into being, dragging
The lopped

Blood-caul of absences.
All night I carpenter

A space for the thing I am given,
A love

Of two wet eyes and a screech.
White spit

Of indifference!
The dark fruits revolve and fall.

The glass cracks across,
The image

Flees and aborts like dropped mercury.

DANIEL MARK EPSTEIN (b. 1948)

The Good Doctors

July: blue sage and lavender heal the earth.
And I have written not a rag of verse
Since April Fool's Day, when the doctors
Said because of an accident of birth,
A stray gene, some rare glitch in the brain
My boy might never reason like a man.
For me it was as if he had died,
Someone I had loved but never known.

Under the harsh lights, none of us could hide.
Because he could not talk or ring a bell
Like other toddlers, put the peg in a hole,
They had removed his body from its soul,
Probing for the mind that binds us all.
And it seemed to me unspeakably cruel
This child, with a great heart and a smile
Everyone who sees must repay in kind,
Should lack sufficient wit to tell—
In this world of falsehood and delusion—
Good from evil, wise from senseless men.
It seemed unthinkably cruel,
And I lost the cadence of a season
That April day in my grief, a broken fool.

TOM HEALY (b. 1961)

The Anesthesiologist's Kiss

He was the first
man I knew

with hair on his face.
I remember his beard

almost covering
his lips, then mine.

I remember
white cotton.

He held my chin
and pressed gently.

I tasted tobacco
and rain trickling

past the soft fears
of a five-year old

into the sturdy home
secrets become.

Oh, little rose.
Drift away.

GARDNER MCFALL (b. 1952)

The Scan

We were given these instruments after your birth:
syringe, Tegaderm, Heparin flush.
This morning, I found them behind the file cabinet.
Dare I throw them out?
I am a superstitious girl.

When I stood in the parted door and gave you up
for the scan, anaesthetized, dye-injected,
your one-year-old body sang
its sweet, green galaxy of bone.
In the corridor, children sat tethered to IVs,

one in a party dress, incongruous as her lack of hair.
Slumped in your room's black corner,
I thought: nothing can save us
unbelievers. I am not like Abraham.

Yet a voice entreated:
Come with me—just this far.
I went to the cool, metal table,
where you lay in the dark.
Haven't I always taken care of her?

Isn't she still here?
When I looked,
I had to say yes,
even as the clicking machine
aimed at your chest.

Robert Frost (1874–1963)

'Out, Out—'

The buzz-saw snarled and rattled in the yard
And made dust and dropped stove-length sticks of wood,
Sweet-scented stuff when the breeze drew across it.
And from there those that lifted eyes could count
Five mountain ranges one behind the other
Under the sunset far into Vermont.
And the saw snarled and rattled, snarled and rattled,
As it ran light, or had to bear a load.
And nothing happened: day was all but done.
Call it a day, I wish they might have said
To please the boy by giving him the half hour
That a boy counts so much when saved from work.
His sister stood beside him in her apron
To tell them "Supper." At that word, the saw,
As if to prove saws know what supper meant,
Leaped out at the boy's hand, or seemed to leap—
He must have given the hand. However it was,
Neither refused the meeting. But the hand!
The boy's first outcry was a rueful laugh,
As he swung toward them holding up the hand
Half in appeal, but half as if to keep
The life from spilling. Then the boy saw all—
Since he was old enough to know, big boy
Doing a man's work, though a child at heart—
He saw all was spoiled. "Don't let him cut my hand off—
The doctor, when he comes. Don't let him, sister!"
So. But the hand was gone already.
The doctor put him in the dark of ether.
He lay and puffed his lips out with his breath.
And then—the watcher at his pulse took fright.
No one believed. They listened to his heart.
Little—less—nothing!—and that ended it.
No more to build on there. And they, since they
Were not the one dead, turned to their affairs.

A. A. MILNE (1882–1956)

Rice Pudding

What is the matter with Mary Jane?
She's crying with all her might and main,
And she won't eat her dinner—rice pudding again—
What *is* the matter with Mary Jane?

What is the matter with Mary Jane?
I've promised her dolls and a daisy-chain,
And a book about animals—all in vain—
What *is* the matter with Mary Jane?

What is the matter with Mary Jane?
She's perfectly well, and she hasn't a pain;
But, look at her, now she's beginning again!—
What *is* the matter with Mary Jane?

What is the matter with Mary Jane?
I've promised her sweets and a ride in the train,
And I've begged her to stop for a bit and explain—
What *is* the matter with Mary Jane?

What is the matter with Mary Jane?
She's perfectly well, and she hasn't a pain,
And it's lovely rice pudding for dinner again!—
What *is* the matter with Mary Jane?

PHILIP LEVINE (b. 1928)

Night Thoughts Over a Sick Child

Numb, stiff, broken by no sleep,
I keep night watch. Looking for
signs to quiet fear, I creep
closer to his bed and hear
his breath come and go, holding
my own as if my own were
all I paid. Nothing I bring,
say, or do has meaning here.

Outside, ice crusts on river
and pond; wild hare come to my
door pacified by torture.
No less ignorant than they
of what grips and why, I am
moved to prayer, the quaint gestures
which ennoble beyond shame
only the mute listener.

No one hears. A dry wind shifts
dry snow, indifferently;
the roof, rotting beneath drifts,
sighs and holds. Terrified by
sleep, the child strives toward
consciousness and the known pain.
If it were mine by one word
I would not save any man,

myself or the universe
at such cost: reality.
Heir to an ancestral curse
though fallen from Judah's tree,
I take up into my arms my hopes,
my son, for what it's worth give
bodily warmth. When he escapes
his heritage, then what have

I left but false remembrance
and the name? Against that day
there is no armor or stance,
only the frail dignity
of surrender, which is all
that can separate me now
or then from the dumb beast's fall,
unseen in the frozen snow.

MICHAEL RYAN (b. 1946)

TV Room at the Children's Hospice

Red-and-green leather-helmeted
maniacally grinning motorcyclists
crash at all angles
on Lev Smith's pajama top

and when his chocolate ice cream
dumps like a mud slide down its front
he smiles, not maniacally, still nauseous
from chemotherapy and bald already.

Lev is six but sat still four hours
all afternoon with IVs in his arms,
his grandma tells everyone. Marcie
is nine and was born with no face.

One profile has been built in increments
with surgical plastic and skin grafts
and the other looks like fudge.
Tomorrow she's having an eye moved.

She finds a hand-mirror in the toy box
and maybe for the minute I watch
she sees nothing she doesn't expect.
Ruth Borthnott's son, Richard,

cracked his second vertebra
at diving practice eight weeks ago,
and as Ruth describes getting the news
by telephone (shampoo suds plopped

all over the notepad she tried
to write on) she smiles like Lev Smith
at his ice cream, smiles also saying
Richard's on a breathing machine,

if he makes it he'll be quadriplegic,
she's there in intensive care every day
at dawn. The gameshow-shrill details
of a Hawaiian vacation for two

and surf teasing the ankles
of the couple on a moonlit beach walk
keep drawing her attention
away from our conversation.

I say it's amazing how life can change
from one second to the next,
and with no apparent disdain
for this dismal platitude,

she nods yes, and yes again
at the game show's svelte assistant
petting a dinette set, and yes
to Lev Smith's grandma

who has appeared beside her
with microwaved popcorn
blooming like a huge
cauliflower from its tin.

MICHAEL SALCMAN (b. 1946)

Medulloblastoma

I hear you're writing a thesis
on the deaths of children expressed in poems.
Perhaps you haven't seen them die yourself
and if you did might forego the subject.

I'm writing to tell you how
the crusts of their scalps become very dry
after chemo and the tiny hairs left behind
curl like watch springs.

They are the first to know—
their eyes glimmering with knowledge.
It's useless to tiptoe around their beds
to whisper and tell them lies.
Their dying is slow
and they see it from a long way off.

LISEL MUELLER (b. 1924)

Epilepsy, Petit Mal

There are times, each day, when their child leaves them—
briefly, for half a minute perhaps—
though she remains standing among them
with the toy or book she is holding.
Her body goes stiff, her pupils lock in position.
She cannot see them. All they can do is wait
until she is given back to them.
Then they ask her where she has been
and she answers, surprised, that she has been with them
the whole time. But they don't believe her;
they think she guards some fantastic secret,
a momentary vision of heaven
so intense that it stuns her. They cannot believe
the alternative, which is nothing—
these mock-deaths, over and over, for nothing.

GABRIEL FRIED (b. 1974)

The Circumcision

Days after that first hurt (when he was first
not with us and we first awaited his return),

his foreskin crept back up him like evening
creeps: unnoticed and then all at once upon its bit

of scenery. Though what should we have hoped
to find beneath the bloody gauze but what will be

his private self recovered? What scars
there are concealed until the sun goes down,

and one by one they permeate his night like stars—

Robert Louis Stevenson (1850–1894)

The Land of Counterpane

When I was sick and lay a-bed,
I had two pillows at my head,
And all my toys beside me lay
To keep me happy all the day.

And sometimes for an hour or so
I watched my leaden soldiers go,
With different uniforms and drills,
Among the bed-clothes, through the hills;

And sometimes sent my ships in fleets
All up and down among the sheets;
Or brought my trees and houses out,
And planted cities all about.

I was the giant great and still
That sits upon the pillow-hill,
And sees before him, dale and plain,
The pleasant land of counterpane.

VI.

LOOKING INSIDE:
PROCEDURES, SURGICAL & DIAGNOSTIC

Bob Hicok (b. 1960)

Surgery

Masked, they cut you, peel back
your skin for the legend of light
to enter your body. In this moment
they love you. You'll know this
years from now, when beating a rug
you feel their hands inside you,
a shock of warmth, invasion of concern,
as if you were back on the table
but awake and aware of the fear
dilating their eyes. How else can it be
for the strangers who take your breath,
contain it in a machine and give it back,
its meter undisturbed? They cut to flaw,
down to a blue tumor the size of an olive.
As they do they think of time, how little
it takes for the riotously dividing cells
to reach blood, to enter the cosmos
of a body and travel to another organ,
another world, advancing cancer's
parasitical flowering. Finally they try
to erase any sign they were there,
stitch and staple where they've cut.
If done well it's like walking backward
across a newly mopped floor. There
are only a few clues, in this case
a scar and the fact on any trivial day
                                        you're still alive.

Thomas Lux (b. 1946)

Upon Seeing an Ultrasound Photo of an Unborn Child

Tadpole, it's not time yet to nag you
about college (though I have some thoughts
on that), baseball (ditto), or abstract
principles. Enjoy your delicious,
soupy womb-warmth, do some rolls and saults
(it'll be too crowded soon), delight in your early
dreams—which no one will attempt to analyze.
For now: may your toes blossom, your fingers
lengthen, your sexual organs grow (too soon
to tell which yet) sensitive, your teeth
form their buds in their forming jawbone, your already
booming heart expand (literally
now, metaphorically later); O your spine,
eyebrows, nape, knees, fibulae,
lungs, lips... But your soul,
dear child: I don't see it here, when
does that come in, whence? Perhaps God,
and your mother, and even I—we'll all contribute
and you'll learn yourself to coax it
from wherever: your soul, which holds your bones
together and lets you live
on earth.—Fingerling, sidecar, nubbin,
I'm waiting, it's me, Dad,
I'm out here. You already know
where Mom is. I'll see you more directly
upon arrival. You'll recognize
me—I'll be the tall-seeming, delighted
blond guy, and I'll have
your nose.

MICHAEL SALCMAN (b. 1946)

Dr. Williams Delivers a Baby

Dr. Williams was making his rounds:
one dilapidated house, then another,
powdered oxygen on the aluminum siding,
brown shingles on the roofs.
In between visits, he'd sit in his car
a notebook on his lap and arrange words—
instruments on a surgical tray—
uterine sounds blunt as tire-irons,
scalpels sharper than paper.
Often a cry from within the house
would bring him running past its yard,
past a tomato plant or wheelbarrow or red hen,
things he took in as he sprang
up the porch steps, hoping the family
was already in the parlor, had put the kettle on,
had found clean towels and disinfectant
to swab the wound or welcome the crowning head.
He put down his old-fashioned doctor's bag,
a satchel peaked like a dormer at both ends,
his initials stamped in gold, long ago faded,
and took off his wool overcoat. Tonight,
he noted the burdened bookshelves,
responsible chair, the goose-necked reading lamp,
the desk loaded with papers, writing tools
and a folding pince-nez: the father
was a professor or writer of some degree,
who could afford both coal and electric.
He suspected they were Jewish, the mother
of German ancestry, the father Sephardic—
but had no reason to know. In truth
he had only a cursory familiarity with their tribe
and knew no Hebrew. But the mother's cry?
Soon, it was going to be soon. He timed her pain
until a dark spot between her labia grew
and it was time to prep and drape her;

then he encouraged the head with a gloved hand
turned the shoulders and delivered the rest.
Dr. Williams told the father it looked like a writer,
this noisy boy, vigorous and exploring.
They would name him Allen.

William Jay Smith (b. 1918)

A Picture of Her Bones

I saw her pelvic bones one April day
After her fall—
Without their leap, without their surge or sway—
I saw her pelvic bones in cold x-ray
After her fall.
She lay in bed; the night before she'd lain
On a mat of leaves, black boulders shining
Between the trees, trees that in rain pitched every which way
Below the crumbling wall,
Making shadows where no shadows were,
Writing black on white, white on black,
As in X-ray,
While rain came slowly down, and gray
Mist rolled up from the valley.
How still, how far away
That scene is now: the car door
Swinging open above her in the night,
A black tongue hanging over
That abyss, saying nothing into the night,
Saying only that white is black and black is white,
Saying only that there was nothing to say.
No blood, no sound,
No sign of hurt nor harm, nothing in disarray,
Slow rain like tears (the tears have dried away).
I held her bare bones in my hands
While swathed in hospital white she lay;
And hold them still, and still they move
As, tall and proud, she strides today,
The sweet grass brushing her thighs,
A whole wet orchard mirrored in her eyes;—
Or move against me here—
With all their lilt, their spring and surge and sway—
As once they did that other April day
Before her fall.

JO MCDOUGALL (b. 1935)

Mammogram

"They're benign," the radiologist says,
pointing to specks on the x-ray
that look like dust motes
stopped cold in their dance.
His words take my spine like flame.
I suddenly love
the radiologist, the nurse, my paper gown,
the vapid print on the dressing room wall.
I pull on my radiant clothes.
I step out into the Hanging Gardens, the Taj Mahal,
the Niagara Falls of the parking lot.

L. E. Sissman (1928–1976)

Negatives

Hello, black skull. How privily you shine
In all my negatives, white pupils mine
Stock-staring forward under the white shock
Of straw, the surrogate for a forelock
To tug and be made free of Schattenland,
Where dusty Freiherren and Freifrauen stand
About apart in independent pools
Of absolute aphosis by the rules
That govern all reversals. Au contraire,
My awesome, glossy X-rays lay me bare
In whited spades: my skull glows like a moon
Hewn, like a button, out of vivid bone;
The tubular members of my rib cage gleam
Like tortile billets of aluminum;
My hand shines, frozen, like a white batwing
Caught in a strobe. The ordinary thing—
The photo-studio-cabinet-portrait shot,
The positive, quite empty of the not-
So-prepossessing characteristics of
Its subject, featly lighted from above
To maximize the massif of the brow
And minimize the blunt thrust of the prow
Above the smiling teeth clamped on a pipe
In smoking, stiff, still smugness, overripe
To fall—is the extraordinary thing.
When I am dead, my coroners will bring
Not my true bills, those rigorous negatives,
Nor those transparently pure fluorographs,
But this dishonest botch in evidence.
Ecco! they'll say, keeping the wolf far hence.

FLOYD SKLOOT (b. 1947)

Sway

I lie back on the narrow bed
and do not know what to do
with my hands. A woman
looms above me, fitting two
chocks tight against my head,
and warns me yet again
not to move. Earphones hiss.
I close my eyes before
beginning to slip
into the magnet's bore.
Soon I hear faint music play
beneath the MRI's
jackhammer rattle. "Sway,"
by Dean Martin, and I
feel its mambo rhythm take
hold down through my toes.
It is all I can do to make
them be still as Dino's
soused-sounding baritone
fills my brain. I need to sing
along now. I have known
this song, from the first *bing*
bing of the chorus to the last
mellow *now*, since learning
the lyrics as a boy whose vast
fantasies included turning
himself into a crooner. I am
in a bath of sense, memory,
and dye. My brain scan
must be lit up like a night sky
by the Northern Lights. But no,
it is not that kind of test,
and then the music stops so
I can hear that the next

phase will last fifteen
minutes, that I have done
very well so far, and please
remember to be still again.

DANIEL HOFFMAN (1923–2013)

Brainwaves

When his head has been wired with a hundred electrodes
Pricked under the skin of his scalp and leading
Into the drum of intricate coils
Where brainwaves stimulate motion

In a finger so sensitive that it can trace
The patterns of idiosyncracy
Which, without his knowing or willing,
Are the actions of his mind,

He is told to lie down on the cot and the current
Begins to flow from his brain through the hidden
Transistors. The needles on the dial veer.
The finger makes a design.

The attendant is reading the dials: no more
Input than from a distant star,
Its energy pulsing for millions of years
To reach the electroscope's cell.

He lies there thinking of nothing, his head
Hurting a little in so many places
He can't tell where. If the current reverses
Direction he'd be in shock,

But the pulsing of twitches and their subsidings
Flow toward squared paper. Is it good
For a man to be made aware that his soul
Is an electric contraption,

The source of his dreams a wavering voltage
From a battery cell—such a piece of work
That the stars in their circuits are driven through space
By an analogue of its plan?

DANNIE ABSE (b. 1923)

The Stethoscope

Through it,
over young women's abdomens tense,
I have heard the sound of creation
and, in a dead man's chest, the silence
    before creation began.

Should I
pray therefore? Hold this instrument in awe
and aloft a procession of banners?
Hang this thing in the interior
    of a cold, mushroom-dark church?

Should I
kneel before it, chant an apophthegm
from a small text? Mimic priest or rabbi,
the swaying noises of religious men?
    Never! Yet I could praise it.

I should
by doing so celebrate my own ears,
by praising them praise speech at midnight
when men become philosophers;
    laughter of the sane and insane;

night cries
of injured creatures, wide-eyed or blind;
moonlight sonatas on a needle;
lovers with doves in their throats; the wind
    travelling from where it began.

SANDRA M. GILBERT (b. 1936)

Colonoscopy Sonnet

On the news tonight, a presidential
colonoscopy—a tale of how
for three whole hours the chief exec of trouble
handed trouble to his vice (although
no double trouble came), but then no more
details revealed: no bacterial armies
multiplying in a flare of war
among kingly polyps & no kinky creases.

Welcome to the presidential gut,
bubble gum pink, not a spot of shit
(after a quick administrative cleanout)
where global decisions stir & sit in state,
    and the first physician's mighty pointer traces
    only microdrops of blood in secret places.

WILLIAM ERNEST HENLEY (1843–1903)

Operation

You are carried in a basket,
Like a carcase from the shambles,
To the theatre, a cockpit
Where they stretch you on a table.

Then they bid you close your eyelids,
And they mask you with a napkin,
And the anæsthetic reaches
Hot and subtle through your being.

And you gasp and reel and shudder
In a rushing, swaying rapture,
While the voices at your elbow
Fade—receding—fainter—farther.

Lights about you shower and tumble,
And your blood seems crystallising—
Edged and vibrant, yet within you
Racked and hurried back and forward.

Then the lights grow fast and furious,
And you hear a noise of waters,
And you wrestle, blind and dizzy,
In an agony of effort,

Till a sudden lull accepts you,
And you sound an utter darkness . . .
And awaken . . . with a struggle . . .
On a hushed, attentive audience.

THOMAS LUX (b. 1946)

Harmonic Scalpel

Of all the tools a surgeon holds,
the knife that hums its way
to where the surgeon wants to go, of all the tools,
that's the best. The patient hears
the tune (the anesthesia local) and is soothed.
Sometimes a nurse (oh white
on white and her nylons too!)
will sway to it, though not
the surgeon: his or her
tapping-toe's shoe
is nailed to the floor.
The knife's a radiant singer
but the hand must be steady, still. The harmonic scalpel
sings its way to the heart,
which needs attending to.
It's red, it's blue: boom, boom, boom.
Above, in the operating theater's low-lit balcony,
the medical students,
in loose green pants
and shirts, with hands
learning to find the body's stress
on and beneath the skin,
the medical students kiss,
and, each the other, caress.

KATE KIMBALL (b.1981)

Transfusion

The needle goes in, breaks the skin like jars
of peaches dropped onto the concrete floor
that spilled orange and yellow syrup past
the hands that felt after her. Shattered. Pushed/
away. Her hair was cut and fell in strips
like open hands still trying, feeling, clenched.
The plastic tubing whispers blood through
her flesh, on gurney like the concrete floor.
The blood spills like the orange syrup dripped
from broken jars with peeled and preserved fruit.

CLAUDIA EMERSON (1957–2014)

The X-Rays

By the time they saw what they were looking at
it was already risen into the bones
of her chest. They could show you then the lungs
were white with it; they said it was like salt
in water—that hard to see as separate—
and would be that hard to remove. Like moonlight
dissolved in fog, in the dense web
of vessels. You say now you kept them longer

than you should have, those shadow-photographs
of the closed room of her body—while you
wandered around inside yourself as though
inside another room she had abandoned
to her absence, to barren light and air,
the one indistinguishable from the other.

DANNIE ABSE (b. 1923)

In The Theatre (A true incident)

*"Only a local anaesthetic was given because of the blood pressure
problem. The patient, thus, was fully awake throughout the
operation. But in those days—in 1938, in Cardiff, when I was
Lambert Rogers' dresser—they could not locate a brain tumour
with precision. Too much normal brain tissue was destroyed as
the surgeon searched for it, before he felt the resistance of it . . .
all somewhat hit and miss. One operation I shall never forget . . ."*
        —Dr. Wilfred Abse

Sister saying—'Soon you'll be back in the ward,'
sister thinking—'Only two more on the list,'
the patient saying—'Thank you, I feel fine';
small voices, small lies, nothing untoward,
though, soon, he would blink again and again
because of the fingers of Lambert Rogers,
rash as a blind man's, inside his soft brain.

If items of horror can make a man laugh
then laugh at this: one hour later, the growth
still undiscovered, ticking its own wild time;
more brain mashed because of the probe's braille path;
Lambert Rogers desperate, fingering still;
his dresser thinking, 'Christ! Two more on the list,
a cisternal puncture and a neural cyst.'

Then, suddenly, the cracked record in the brain,
a ventriloquist voice that cried, 'You sod,
leave my soul alone, leave my soul alone,'—
the patient's dummy lips moving to that refrain,
the patient's eyes too wide. And, shocked,
Lambert Rogers drawing out the probe
with nurses, students, sister, petrified.

'Leave my soul alone, leave my soul alone,'
that voice so arctic and that cry so odd
had nowhere else to go—till the antique
gramophone wound down and the words began
to blur and slow, '. . . leave . . . my . . . soul . . . alone . . .'
to cease at last when something other died.
And silence matched the silence under snow.

Frederick Seidel (b. 1936)

At New York Hospital

I enter the center.
I open the book of there.
I leave my clothes in a locker.
I gown myself and scrub in.

Anything is possible that I do.
Cutting a person open
Is possible without pain. An entourage rolls
In a murderous head of state with beautiful big breasts—

Who is already under and extremely nude
On the gurney. Her sheet has slipped off.
Her perfect head has been shaved
Bald. And now a target area

On the top of the skull will
Be painted magenta. Her body is re-wrapped.
Her face gets sealed off. Her crimes against humanity
Will be lasered.

I am a Confederate scout, silence in the forest.
The all eyes and stillness
Of a bird watcher has stumbled on
A Yankee soldier asleep.

The dentist's drill drills a hole and
The drill slips and whines out of control,
But no matter. The electric saw cuts
Out a skullcap of bone.

The helicopter descends from Olympus to within an
Inch of touching down
On the wrinkled surface, when a tool falls incredibly
To the floor and I pick it up and am thanked.

The anesthesiologist for my benefit joyously
Declaims Gerard Manley Hopkins.
The surgeon recites a fervent favorite childhood hymn.
He slaps the monster tenderly to wake her up. Wake up, darling.

VII.

TUMORS, TRAUMA, & TUMULT

STANLEY PLUMLY (b. 1939)

Cancer

Mine, I know, started at a distance
five hundred and twenty light-years away
and fell as stardust into my sleeping mouth,
yesterday, at birth, or that time when I was ten
lying on my back looking up at the cluster
called the Beehive or by its other name
in the constellation Cancer,
the Crab, able to move its nebulae projections
backward and forward, side to side,
in the tumor Hippocrates describes as carcinoma,
from *karkinos*, the analogue, in order to show
what being cancer looks like.
Star, therefore, to start,
like waking on the best day of your life
to feel this living and immortal thing inside you.
You were in love, you were a saint,
you were going to walk the sunlight blessing water,
you were almost word for word forever.
The crown, the throne, the thorn—
now to see the smoke shining in the mirror,
the long half-dark of dark down the hallway inside it.
Now to see what wasn't seen before:
the old loved landscape fading from the window,
the druid soul within the dying tree,
the depth of blue coloring the cornflower,
the birthday-ribbon river of a road,
and the young man who resembles you
opening a door in the half-built house
you helped your father build,
saying, in your voice, come forth.

DAVID FERRY (b. 1924)

At the Hospital

She was the sentence the cancer spoke at last,
Its blurred grammar finally clarified.

ALICIA OSTRIKER (b. 1937)

Nude Descending

Like a bowerbird trailing a beakful of weeds
Like prize ribbons for the very best

The lover, producer
Of another's pleasure

He whom her swollen lips await
Might wing through any day of the decade

A form of health insurance
For which it is never too late

Titanic, silver brush
Hindenburg, of exploding cigars a climax

The watery below, the fiery above
Ashes of print between—pigment between

If the crippled woman were to descend
From her bed, her fortress beyond midnight

Downstairs (*nude/staircase*) to the kitchen
Naked to sit at the table (*writing/thinking*)

She might hear the washer spin like a full orchestra
Complete a cycle like a train crash

Before the fiend would stare through the window
Step smoothly into the kitchen, stop some clocks.

Envy shapes a fig tree in one's breast,
That is bluntly to say a cancer,

That is to say
In a mind, a fertile windy field. A murdered child.

Well then, fear, primarily of falling.
Ebony surf toils on the beach, a glaze

At the same moment I am (*from a cliff*) falling
The kitchen fiend removes his Dior tie

Places his hand over the woman's
And softly says: I am the lover.

Now if the crippled woman began to dance
To pirouette, to rumba

Growling for her child
Her burning page, the devil would be shamed

(*Materialism is not for everyone / Religion is
The extension of politics by other means*)

Would disembody like a wicked smoke
Back to the status of myth

Away he'd streak, blue, into the—
O faun, we would finally call, farewell

O faun, we would faintly faintly call
O faun, we would, we would fondly—

She does not dance. She does not wish
To produce another's pleasure.

They have torn her apart
Into beige rectangles.

MARILYN HACKER (b. 1942)

from Cancer Winter

I woke up, and the surgeon said, "You're cured."
Strapped to the gurney, in the cotton gown
and pants I was wearing when they slid me down
onto the table, made new straps secure
while I stared at the hydra-headed O.R.
lamp, I took in the tall, confident, brown-
skinned man, and the ache I couldn't quite call pain
from where my right breast wasn't anymore
to my armpit. A not-yet-talking head,
I bit dry lips. What else could he have said?
And then my love was there in a hospital coat;
then my old love, still young and very scared.
Then I, alone, graphed clock hands' asymptote
to noon, when I would be wheeled back upstairs.

*

At noon, an orderly wheeled me upstairs
via an elevator hung with Season's
Greetings streamers, bright and false as treason.
The single room the surgeon let us share
the night before the knife was scrubbed and bare
except for blush-pink roses in a vase on
the dresser. Veering through a morphine haze on
the cranked bed, I was avidly aware
of my own breathing, my thirst, that it was over—
the week that ended on this New Year's Eve.
A known hand held, while I sipped, icewater,
afloat between ache, sleep, lover and lover.
The one who stayed would stay; the one would leave.
The hand that held the cup next was my daughter's.

J.D. McClatchy (b. 1945)

Cancer

1.

And then a long senescent cell—though why,
Who knows?—will suddenly refuse to stay
In line, the bucket brigade of proteins meant
To slow or stimulate the tissue's growth
Will stumble, so the cells proliferate
And tumors form while, deep within,
Suppressor genes, mutated, overlook
The widening fault, the manic drive to choke
On itself that fairy tales allot the gnome
Who vainly hammers the broken sword in his cave,
Where malignant cells are shed into the blood
Or lymph, cascading through the body's streams,
Attaching themselves to places where we breathe
And love and think of what cannot be true.

2.

It is as if, the stench intensified
And strong or weak alike now swept away,
The plague in Athens hurried its descent
By fear, a symptom leaving the stricken loath
To fight for life who had defied the great
Spartan ranks themselves, the sight of skin
Inflamed, the thirst, the dripping anus took
Hold of them until, in tears, they broke.
The dead in piles around them, a hecatomb
To gods who, like those mongrel dogs who crave
A corpse they drag to safety through the mud
To feast upon, had disappeared, their dreams,
According to Thucydides, seethed
With images of forsaken, drowning crews.

3.

She had lost the bet, and in her sunken eyes
The birthday she had over and over prayed
To die before was offered like a present.
(Dressed in a party hat, I sat with both
My parents by the bed.) A toast was made.
Through the pleated, angled straw she took in
A burning mouthful of champagne, and rebuked
Her son-in-law for his expensive joke,
Drawing, hairless, an imaginary comb
Through memories of what pleasure anger gave,
Then smiled, "I'd stop all this if only I could."
Even at ten I sensed that she had seen,
Staring at me, what would be bequeathed.
My mother slowly closed her eyes. We knew.

MARC STRAUS (b. 1945)

Luck

Just my luck. I gave up smoking last month
and the doctor says there's a lesion in my lung.

If I'm lucky, he says, it'll be curable.
I tell him the T.V. showed two kids rescued

from a burning building and the reporter said
it's lucky they're alive. So I say, how come

it's lucky they got second degree burns. How come
they were in the building in the first place.

Want to hear about real luck, I say. I have this itch
under my arm. I'll scratch it twice in slow circles

and the lesion in my lung is gone.

DAVID BERGMAN (b. 1950)

A Child's Garden of Curses

I have a little tumor
That's growing from my brain.
It sometimes makes me dizzy,
But never gives me pain.

It casts a little shadow
On a recent MRI
Just out of easy access
Like a well constructed lie.

I'm trying to accept it
Like a neighbor down the street
Who rarely sweeps the sidewalk
And is noisy when I sleep,

But secretly I'm waiting
For that moment when I'll shout
At surgeons like policemen
To run the bastard out.

TERESE SVOBODA (b. 1950)

Hysterical Leg

Betrayed. Saw it off. Instead,
this plank, shimmed straight,
taught taut, all its music

jangled, translated "nought"
by the foreigner, me.
I point, and the able-bodied,

white-coated natives read
only sign language's nadir,
e.g., tears. But not for meaning.

Pain, just another appendage,
drags every step. The horizon
disappears without me.

Tylenol, that pseudo-Scandinavian,
whispers—but what does he say?
The leg goes only so far.

C. P. Cavafy (1863–1933)

The Bandaged Shoulder

He said that he had hurt himself on a wall or that he had fallen.
But there was probably another reason
for the wounded and bandaged shoulder.

With a somewhat abrupt movement,
to bring down from a shelf some
photographs that he wanted to see closely,
the bandage was untied and a little blood ran.

I bandaged the shoulder again, and while bandaging it
I was somewhat slow; because it did not hurt,
and I liked to look at the blood. That
blood was a part of my love.

When he had left, I found in front of the chair,
a bloody rag, from the bandages,
a rag that looked as if it belonged in the garbage;
which I brought up to my lips,
and which I held there for a long time—
the blood of love on my lips.

MIROSLAV HOLUB (1923–1998)

Casualty

They bring us crushed fingers,
mend it, doctor.
They bring burnt-out eyes,
hounded owls of hearts,
they bring a hundred white bodies,
a hundred red bodies,
a hundred black bodies,
mend it, doctor,
on the dishes of ambulances they bring
the madness of blood
the scream of flesh,
the silence of charring,
mend it, doctor.

And while we are suturing
inch after inch,
night after night,
nerve to nerve,
muscle to muscle,
eyes to sight,
they bring in
even longer daggers,
even more thunderous bombs,
even more glorious victories,

idiots.

Sylvia Plath (1932–1963)

The Surgeon at 2 A.M.

The white light is artificial, and hygienic as heaven.
The microbes cannot survive it.
They are departing in their transparent garments, turned aside
From the scalpels and the rubber hands.
The scalded sheet is a snowfield, frozen and peaceful.
The body under it is in my hands.
As usual there is no face. A lump of Chinese white
With seven holes thumbed in. The soul is another light.
I have not seen it; it does not fly up.
Tonight it has receded like a ship's light.

It is a garden I have to do with—tubers and fruits
Oozing their jammy substances,
A mat of roots. My assistants hook them back.
Stenches and colors assail me.
This is the lung-tree.
These orchids are splendid. They spot and coil like snakes.
The heart is a red bell-bloom, in distress.
I am so small
In comparison to these organs!
I worm and hack in a purple wilderness.

The blood is a sunset. I admire it.
I am up to my elbows in it, red and squeaking.
Still is seeps me up, it is not exhausted.
So magical! A hot spring
I must seal off and let fill
The intricate, blue piping under this pale marble.
How I admire the Romans—
Aqeducts, the Baths of Caracalla, the eagle nose!
The body is a Roman thing.
It has shut its mouth on the stone pill of repose.

It is a statue the orderlies are wheeling off.
I have perfected it.
I am left with an arm or a leg,
A set of teeth, or stones
To rattle in a bottle and take home,
And tissues in slices—a pathological salami.
Tonight the parts are entombed in an icebox.
Tomorrow they will swim
In vinegar like saints' relics.
Tomorrow the patient will have a clean, pink plastic limb.

Over one bed in the ward, a small blue light
Announces a new soul. The bed is blue.
Tonight, for this person, blue is a beautiful color.
The angels of morphia have borne him up.
He floats an inch from the ceiling,
Smelling the dawn drafts.
I walk among sleepers in gauze sarcophagi.
The red night lights are flat moons. They are dull with blood.
I am the sun, in my white coat,
Gray faces, shuttered by drugs, follow me like flowers.

FREDERICK SEIDEL (b.1936)

Doctor Love

It was a treatment called
Doctor Love, after the main character.
One of the producers discovered
To our horror a real

Dr. Love who, eerily, by
Pure coincidence, was also a woman
Oncologist trying to identify the gene that causes
Breast cancer. My

Fiction trampolined
Herself right off the treatment page,
Landing not on a movie set or a screen at the multiplex,
But at a teaching hospital in Los Angeles directing

Her lab. If you could identify the gene
That turns the cancer on,
Then maybe you could find a way to turn it off—
And make somebody rich.

She found a gene.
The villain needed to learn which.
He sets the innocent doctor up to
Commit a murder. The story was in such bad taste.

It never made sense.
I was doing rounds in a long white coat
To write the screenplay—playing doctor, doctor love.
Til death do us part, Dr. Catherine Hart,

I will remember you
On the street kissing me hello.
The cherry blossom petals blow—
White coats on rounds

In a soft East River breeze—like glowing fireflies of snow.
Dear Hart, it is spring.
Cutting a person open
Is possible without pain.

ROBERT COOPERMAN (b. 1946)

The Medical Student John Keats Observes Astley Cooper Operate on a Young Boy, Guy's Hospital

The boy smiled through his fear—
brave as only the innocent can be—
while we students crowded,
the amphitheatre hot as the blood
soon to baptize the scalpel.
I'd set bones before, patients sweating,
fainting when the shards snapped back
after that scorching instant.

Now I stood opposite Dr. Cooper,
who had operated scores of times.
But when that lad smiled
as if at Father Christmas,
tears trickled down the surgeon's cheeks.
I saw, for a moment,
my own small brother Tom
squirming on the table,
and wanted to escape
with him riding my back—
the jockey of our childhood races.

Cooper turned away, wiped his face,
and when he turned back
the eyes of a stooping hawk.
At the first incision,
the power of the possessed
levitated that betrayed torso,
but not a scream from lips clamped
in tooth-shattering trust.

"Blame God," Cooper muttered,
"for making flesh fail,
the need for such an insult as this
to thin, pale tissue,
frail enough without the blade."

YEHUDA AMICHAI (1924–2000)

A Pity. We Were Such a Good Invention

They amputated
your thighs from my hips.
As far as I'm concerned, they're always
doctors. All of them.
They dismantled us
from each other. As far as I'm concerned,
they're engineers.
A pity. We were such a good and loving
invention: an airplane made of a man and a woman,
wings and all:
we even got off
the ground a little.
We even flew.

PHILIP APPLEMAN (b. 1926)

Eulogy

That swain in Shakespeare, penning ballads
to his lady's eyebrow: if just once
he could have seen my sweetheart's breasts,
he would have written epics. Oh,
they are so springtime sweet and summer-lilting,
those twin blossoms, I should have found
a painter intimate with tender shades
of pink and cream
to immortalize their harmony.

Because
up there on the seventh floor
they are cutting one of them away,
the one we touched last week and felt
the poisoned pearl.
Now the knives are working, working,
I feel them stabbing through my flesh.
She will come back gray, remembering
to smile, the bandages weeping blood,
her beauty scarred,
her life saved.

I will love her more
than yesterday.

SARAH N. CROSS (b. 1977)

Over the Liver

Lay yourself down
for a sleep. As you drift
we give you conversations
of ocean, sky, mountains.

Once you are departed
only very much still here,
all here, I ask for the knife,
the surface of your skin, glinting

with fine fur, a mole,
hint of your old battles–
where your child was born up
out of you, grown now, now waiting

down the hall in the yellow room
while I press the knife from north
to south, allow blood to come.
From umbilicus to pubis, open:

white fascia, tough like thin bark,
the heft of rectus divided into red,
then deep pink, shining like the inside
of shell washed in salt water, which comes up.

In all the depth of your bone,
bowel, muscle, you are not free:
where you carried your child
now fixed down by tumor.

My hand travels down the sides
of your pelvis and up over the liver
where the cells have spread, small seeds
in the dark angles of your diaphragm.

ANYA SILVER (b. 1968)

To My Body

Open yourself to me.

You have suffered great losses.
Hands have breached your thresholds.
You have delivered the dead
and the living. You have bled.
Your glands, linings, fat,
have been raked
and exhumed. Body—poisoned, cut, burned—
too tired to rise, you've risen.

How easily I used to slip from my wet bathing suits,
leaving slick skins on the bathroom floor.

Even now, oh, body, I will not
believe the evidence, the stitched
flesh and puckered flap.

Our time together is short.
Do not leave me.

VIII.

DOCTORS & OTHER HEALERS

WILLIAM CARLOS WILLIAMS (1883–1963)

Complaint

They call me and I go.
It is a frozen road
past midnight, a dust
of snow caught
in the rigid wheeltracks.
The door opens.
I smile, enter and
shake off the cold.
Here is a great woman
on her side in the bed.
She is sick,
perhaps vomiting,
perhaps laboring
to give birth to
a tenth child. Joy! Joy!
Night is a room
darkened for lovers,
through the jalousies the sun
has sent one golden needle!
I pick the hair from her eyes
and watch her misery
with compassion.

W. H. AUDEN (1907–1973)

Give Me A Doctor

Give me a doctor, partridge-plump,
Short in the leg and broad in the rump,
An endomorph with gentle hands,
Who'll never make absurd demands
That I abandon all my vices,
Nor pull a long face in a crisis,
But with a twinkle in his eye
Will tell me that I have to die.

GEOFFREY CHAUCER (c.1343–1400)

The Physician

There also was among us a PHYSICIAN,
None like him in this world, no competition,
To speak of medicine and surgery.
He was well grounded in astrology:
He tended patients specially in hours
When natural magic had its greatest powers,
For he could tell by which stars would ascend
What talisman would help his patient mend.
He knew the cause of every malady
Whether from hot, cold, wet, or dry it be,
And of each humor what the symptoms were.
He truly was a fine practitioner.
And once he knew a malady's root cause
He'd give the cure without a further pause,
For readily apothecaries heeded
When there were drugs or medicines he needed,
That profit might be shared by everyone
(Their fellowship not recently begun).
The ancient Aesculapius he knew,
And Dioscorides and Rufus too,
Hali and Galen, old Hippocrates,
Serapion, Avicenna, Rhazes,
Gaddesden, Damascenus, Constantine,
Bernard and Averroes and Gilbertine.
His diet was as measured as could be,
Being not one of superfluity
But greatly nourishing as well as prudent.
He hardly could be called a Bible student.
He decked himself in scarlet and in azure,
With taffeta and silk. Yet he'd demure
If something might necessitate expense;
He saved his gains from times of pestilence,
For gold's a cordial, so the doctors say.
That's why he loved gold in a special way.

OLIVER WENDELL HOLMES (1809–1894)

A Poem for the Meeting of the American Medical Association at New York, May 5, 1853

I hold a letter in my hand,—
    A flattering letter, more's the pity,—
By some contriving junto planned,
    And signed *per order of Committee*;
It touches every tenderest spot,—
    My patriotic predilections,
My well-known—something—don't ask what,—
    My poor old songs, my kind affections.

They make a feast on Thursday next,
    And hope to make the feasters merry;
They own they're something more perplexed
    For poets than for port and sherry;—
They want the men of—(word torn out);
    Our friends will come with anxious faces
(To see our blankets off, no doubt,
    And trot us out and show our paces).
They hint that papers by the score
    Are rather musty kind of rations;
They don't exactly mean a bore,
    But only trying to the patience;
That such as—you know who I mean—
    Distinguished for their—what d' ye call 'em—
Should bring the dews of Hippocrene
    To sprinkle on the faces solemn.

—The same old story: that's the chaff
    To catch the birds that sing the ditties;
Upon my soul, it makes me laugh
    To read these letters from Committees!
They're all *so* loving and *so* fair,—
    All for *your* sake such kind compunction;
'T would save your carriage half its wear
    To touch its wheels with such an unction!

Why, who am I, to lift me here
    And beg such learned folk to listen,
To ask a smile, or coax a tear
    Beneath these stoic lids to glisten?
As well might some arterial thread
    Ask the whole frame to feel it gushing,
While throbbing fierce from heel to head
    The vast aortic tide was rushing.

As well some hair-like nerve might strain
    To set its special streamlet going,
While through the myriad-channelled brain
    The burning flood of thought was flowing;
Or trembling fibre strive to keep
    The springing haunches gathered shorter,
While the scourged racer, leap on leap,
    Was stretching through the last hot quarter!

Ah me! you take the bud that came
Self-sown in your poor garden's borders,
And hand it to the stately dame
    That florists breed for, all she orders.
She thanks you,—it was kindly meant,—
    (A pale affair, not worth the keeping,)—
Good morning; and your bud is sent
    To join the tea-leaves used for sweeping.
Not always so, kind hearts and true,—
    For such I know are round me beating;
Is not the bud I offer you,
    Fresh gathered for the hour of meeting—
Pale though its outer leaves may be,
    Rose-red in all its inner petals,
Where the warm life we cannot see—
    The life of love that gave it—settles.

We meet from regions far away,
    Like rills from distant mountains streaming;
The sun is on Francisco's bay,
    O'er Chesapeake the lighthouse gleaming;
While summer girds the still bayou
    In chains of bloom, her bridal token,
Monadnock sees the sky grow blue,
    His crystal bracelet yet unbroken.

Yet Nature bears the selfsame heart
    Beneath her russet-mantled bosom
As where, with burning lips apart,
    She breathes and white magnolias blossom;
The selfsame founts her chalice fill
    With showery sunlight running over,
On fiery plain and frozen hill,
    On myrtle-beds and fields of clover.

I give you *Home*! its crossing lines
    United in one golden suture,
And showing every day that shines
    The present growing to the future,—
A flag that bears a hundred stars
    In one bright ring, with love for centre,
Fenced round with white and crimson bars
    No prowling treason dares to enter!

O brothers, home may be a word
    To make affection's living treasure—
The wave an angel might have stirred—
    A stagnant pool of selfish pleasure;
HOME! It is where the day-star springs
    And where the evening sun reposes,
Where'er the eagle spreads his wings,
    From northern pines to southern roses!

WALT WHITMAN (1819–1892)

The Wound-Dresser

1

An old man bending I come among new faces,
Years looking backward resuming in answer to children,
Come tell us old man, as from young men and maidens that love me,
(Arous'd and angry, I'd thought to beat the alarum, and urge relentless war,
But soon my fingers fail'd me, my face droop'd and I resign'd myself,
To sit by the wounded and soothe them, or silently watch the dead;)
Years hence of these scenes, of these furious passions, these chances,
Of unsurpass'd heroes, (was one side so brave? the other was equally brave;)
Now be witness again, paint the mightiest armies of earth,
Of those armies so rapid so wondrous that saw you to tell us?
What stays with you latest and deepest? of curious panics,
Of hard-fought engagements or sieges tremendous what deepest remains?

2

O maidens and young men I love and that love me,
What you ask of my days those the strangest and sudden your talking
    recalls,
Soldier alert I arrive after a long march cover'd with sweat and dust,
In the nick of time I come, plunge in the fight, loudly shout in the rush
    of successful charge,
Enter the captur'd works—yet lo, like a swift-running river they fade,
Pass and are gone they fade—I dwell not on soldiers' perils or soldiers' joys,
(Both I remember well—many the hardships, few the joys, yet I was
    content.)

But in silence, in dreams' projections,
While the world of gain and appearance and mirth goes on,
So soon what is over forgotten, and waves wash the imprints off the sand,
With hinged knees returning I enter the doors, (while for you up there,
Whoever you are, follow without noise and be of strong heart.)

Bearing the bandages, water and sponge,
Straight and swift to my wounded I go,
Where they lie on the ground after the battle brought in,
Where their priceless blood reddens the grass the ground,
Or to the rows of the hospital tent, or under the roof'd hospital,
To the long rows of cots up and down each side I return,
To each and all one after another I draw near, not one do I miss,
An attendant follows holding a tray, he carries a refuse pail,
Soon to be fill'd with clotted rags and blood, emptied, and fill'd again.

I onward go, I stop,
With hinged knees and steady hand to dress wounds,
I am firm with each, the pangs are sharp yet unavoidable,
One turns to me his appealing eyes—poor boy! I never knew you,
Yet I think I could not refuse this moment to die for you, if that would
    save you.

3
On, on I go, (open doors of time! open hospital doors!)
The crush'd head I dress, (poor crazed hand tear not the bandage away,)
The neck of the cavalry-man with the bullet through and through I
    examine,
Hard the breathing rattles, quite glazed already the eye, yet life struggles
    hard,
(Come sweet death! be persuaded O beautiful death!
In mercy come quickly.)

From the stump of the arm, the amputated hand,
I undo the clotted lint, remove the slough, wash off the matter and blood,
Back on his pillow the soldier bends with curv'd neck and side-falling head,
His eyes are closed, his face is pale, he dares not look on the bloody stump,
And has not yet look'd on it.

I dress a wound in the side, deep, deep,
But a day or two more, for see the frame all wasted and sinking,
And the yellow-blue countenance see.

I dress the perforated shoulder, the foot with the bullet-wound,
Cleanse the one with a gnawing and putrid gangrene, so sickening, so
    offensive,
While the attendant stands behind aside me holding the tray and pail.

I am faithful, I do not give out,
The fractur'd thigh, the knee, the wound in the abdomen,
These and more I dress with impassive hand, (yet deep in my breast a
    fire, a burning flame.)

4
Thus in silence in dreams' projections,
Returning, resuming, I thread my way through the hospitals,
The hurt and wounded I pacify with soothing hand,
I sit by the restless all the dark night, some are so young,
Some suffer so much, I recall the experience sweet and sad,
(Many a soldier's loving arms about this neck have cross'd and rested,
Many a soldier's kiss dwells on these bearded lips.)

WILLIAM ERNEST HENLEY (1849–1903)

Lady-Probationer

Some three, or five, or seven, and thirty years;
A Roman nose; a dimpling double-chin;
Dark eyes and shy that, ignorant of sin,
Are yet acquainted, it would seem, with tears;
A comely shape; a slim, high-coloured hand,
Graced, rather oddly, with a signet ring;
A bashful air, becoming everything;
A well-bred silence always at command.
Her plain print gown, prim cap, and bright steel chain
Look out of place on her, and I remain
Absorbed in her, as in a pleasant mystery.
Quick, skilful, quiet, soft in speech and touch . . .
'Do you like nursing?' 'Yes, Sir, very much.'
Somehow, I rather think she has a history.

EDGAR LEE MASTERS (1868–1950)

Doctor Meyers

No other man, unless it was Doc Hill,
Did more for people in this town than I.
And all the weak, the halt, the improvident
And those who could not pay flocked to me.
I was good-hearted, easy Doctor Meyers.
I was healthy, happy, in comfortable fortune,
Blest with a congenial mate, my children raised,
All wedded, doing well in the world.
And then one night, Minerva, the poetess,
Came to me in her trouble, crying.
I tried to help her out—she died—
They indicted me, the newspapers disgraced me,
My wife perished of a broken heart.
And pneumonia finished me.

Mrs. Meyers

He protested all his life long
The newspapers lied about him villainously;
That he was not at fault for Minerva's fall,
But only tried to help her.
Poor soul so sunk in sin he could not see
That even trying to help her, as he called it,
He had broken the law human and divine.
Passers by, an ancient admonition to you:
If your ways would be ways of pleasantness,
And all your pathways peace,
Love God and keep his commandments.

E. A. ROBINSON (1869–1935)

How Annandale Went Out

"They called it Annandale—and I was there
To flourish, to find words, and to attend:
Liar, physician, hypocrite, and friend,
I watched him; and the sight was not so fair
As one or two that I have seen elsewhere:
An apparatus not for me to mend—
A wreck, with hell between him and the end,
Remained of Annandale; and I was there.

"I knew the ruin as I knew the man;
So put the two together, if you can,
Remembering the worst you know of me.
Now view yourself as I was, on the spot—
With a slight kind of engine. Do you see?
Like this . . . You wouldn't hang me? I thought not."

WALLACE STEVENS (1879–1955)

The Doctor of Geneva

The doctor of Geneva stamped the sand
That lay impounding the Pacific swell,
Patted his stove-pipe hat and tugged his shawl.

Lacustrine man had never been assailed
By such long-rolling opulent cataracts,
Unless Racine or Bossuet held the like.

He did not quail. A man so used to plumb
The multifarious heavens felt no awe
Before these visible, voluble delugings,

Which yet found means to set his simmering mind
Spinning and hissing with oracular
Notations of the wild, the ruinous waste,

Until the steeples of his city clanked and sprang
In an unburgherly apocalypse.
The doctor used his handkerchief and sighed.

E. E. CUMMINGS (1894–1962)

from One Times One

pity this busy monster, manunkind,

not. Progress is a comfortable disease:
your victum (death and life safely beyond)

plays with the bigness of his littleness
—electrons deify one razorblade
into a mountainrange; lenses extend

unwish through curving wherewhen until unwish
returns on its unself.
                        A world of made
is not a world of born—pity poor flesh

and trees,poor stars and stones,but never this
fine specimen of hypermagical

ultraomnipotence. We doctors know

a hopeless case if—listen: there's a hell
of a good universe next door; let's go

RAMON GUTHRIE (1896–1973)

Red-Headed Intern, Taking Notes

Do you been or did you never? Ha!
Speakless, can you flex your omohyoid
and whinny ninety-nine? Quick now,
can you recall your grandmother's maiden name
six times rapidly? Have you a phobia of spiders?
Only fairly large and brown ones
dropping from the ceiling?
Does this happen often, would you say?
(Nurse, clamp the necrometer when I say when.
If he passes out, tickle his nose with a burning feather
and tweak his ears counterclockwise.)
And tularemia? No recent intercourse
with a rabbit?
      (Lash him firmly to the stretcher
      and store him in the ghast house for the night.)

The Doctor Who Sits at the Bedside of a Rat

The doctor who sits at the bedside of a rat
    Obtains real answers—a paw twitch,
    An ear tremor, a gain or loss of weight.
    No problem as to which
    Is temper and which is true.
    What a rat feels, a rat will do.

Concomitantly then, the doctor who sits
    At the bedside of a rat
    Asks real questions, as befits
    The place, like Where did that potassium go, not What
    Do you think of Willie Mays or the weather?
    So rat and doctor may converse together.

ROBERT HAYDEN (1913–1980)

Witch Doctor

I
He dines alone surrounded by reflections
of himself. Then after sleep and benzedrine
descends the Cinquecento stair his magic
wrought from hypochondria of the well-
to-do and nagging deathwish of the poor;
swirls on smiling genuflections of
his liveried chauffeur into a crested
lilac limousine, the cynosure
of mousey neighbors tittering behind
Venetian blinds and half afraid of him
and half admiring his outrageous flair.

II
Meanwhile his mother, priestess in gold lamé,
precedes him to the quondam theater
now Israel Temple of the Highest Alpha,
where the bored, the sick, the alien, the tired
await euphoria. With deadly vigor
she prepares the way for mystery
and lucre. Shouts in blues-contralto, "He's
God's dictaphone of all-redeeming truth.
Oh he's the holyweight champeen who's come
to give the knockout lick to your bad luck;
say he's the holyweight champeen who's here
to deal a knockout punch to your hard luck."

III

Reposing on cushions of black leopard skin,
he telephones instructions for a long
slow drive across the park that burgeons now
with spring and sailors. Peers questingly
into the green fountainous twilight, sighs
and turns the gold-plate dial to Music For
Your Dining-Dancing Pleasure. Smoking Egyptian
cigarettes rehearses in his mind
a new device that he must use tonight.

IV

Approaching Israel Temple, mask in place,
he hears ragtime allegros of a "Song
of Zion" that becomes when he appears
a hallelujah wave for him to walk.
His mother and a rainbow-surpliced cordon
conduct him choiring to the altar-stage,
and there he kneels and seems to pray before
a lighted Jesus painted sealskin-brown.
Then with a glittering flourish he arises,
turns, gracefully extends his draperied arms:
"Israelites, true Jews, O found lost tribe
of Israel, receive my blessing now.
Selah, selah." He feels them yearn toward him
as toward a lover, exults before the image
of himself their trust gives back. Stands as though
in meditation, letting their eyes caress
his garments jewelled and chatoyant, cut
to fall, to flow from his tall figure
dramatically just so. Then all at once
he sways, quivers, gesticulates as if
to ward off blows or kisses, and when he speaks
again he utters wildering vocables,
hypnotic no-words planned (and never failing)

to enmesh his flock in theopathic tension.
Cries of eudaemonic pain attest
his artistry. Behind the mask he smiles.
And now in subtly altering light he chants
and sinuously trembles, chants and trembles
while convulsive energies of eager faith
surcharge the theater with power of
their own, a power he has counted on
and for a space allows to carry him.
Dishevelled antiphons proclaim the moment
his followers all day have hungered for,
but which is his alone.
He signals: tambourines begin, frenetic
drumbeat and glissando. He dances from the altar,
robes hissing, flaring, shimmering; down aisles
where mantled guardsmen intercept wild hands
that arduously strain to clutch his vestments,
he dances, dances, ensorcelled and aloof,
the fervid juba of God as lover, healer,
conjurer. And of himself as God.

DANNIE ABSE (b. 1923)

Song for Pythagoras

White coat and purple coat
    a sleeve from both he sews.
That white is always stained with blood,
    that purple by the rose.

And phantom rose and blood most real
    compose a hybrid style;
white coat and purple coat
    few men can reconcile.

White coat and purple coat
    can each be worn in turn
but in the white a man will freeze
    and in the purple burn.

JOHN STONE (1936–2008)

Talking to the Family

My white coat waits in the corner
like a father.
I will wear it to meet the sister
in her white shoes and organza dress
in the live of winter,

the milkless husband
holding the baby.

I will tell them.

They will put it together
and take it apart.
Their voices will buzz.
The cut ends of their nerves
will curl.

I will take off the coat,
drive home,
and replace the light bulb in the hall.

ANNE SEXTON (1928–1974)

Doctors

They work with herbs
and penicillin.
They work with gentleness
and the scalpel.
They dig out the cancer,
close an incision
and say a prayer
to the poverty of the skin.
They are not Gods
though they would like to be;
they are only a human
trying to fix up a human.
Many humans die.
They die like the tender,
palpitating berries
in November.
But all along the doctors remember:
First do no harm.
They would kiss if it would heal.
It would not heal.

If the doctors cure
then the sun sees it.
If the doctors kill
then the earth hides it.
The doctors should fear arrogance
more than cardiac arrest.
If they are too proud,
and some are,
then they leave home on horseback
but God returns them on foot.

FREDERICK SEIDEL (b. 1936)

Holly Andersen

I describe you.
I have a chart to.
I hold your
Heart. I feel.

The motor
Of your life
Is not diseased or weak
Or real until

I stress it from the
Outside, how
You test anyone before you
Find them true.

Totally in
Your power,
The stethoscope
Puts its taproot to your chest, and flowers.

The miles of
Treadmill agnostically
Takes core samples.
The bolus which jump-starts us back to life is love.

The light leaps and is living
On the screen
As the mine-detector mechanism
Looks for mines.

Take a deep breath.
You stopped smoking cigarettes.
Breathe out through your mouth.
How many years ago.

We are made of years
That keep on living.
We are made of tears
That as your doctor I can't cry.

JAMES TATE (b. 1943)

On the Subject of Doctors

I like to see doctors cough.
What kind of human being
would grab all your money
just when you're down?
I'm not saying they enjoy this:
"Sorry, Mr. Rodriguez, that's it,
no hope! You might as well
hand over your wallet." Hell no,
they'd rather be playing golf
and swapping jokes about our feet.

Some of them smoke marijuana
and are alcoholics, and their moral
turpitude is famous: who gets to see
most sex organs in the world? Not
poets. With the hours they keep
they need drugs more than anyone.
Germ city, there's no hope
looking down those fire-engine throats.
They're bound to get sick themselves
sometime; and I happen to be there
myself in a high fever
taking my plastic medicine seriously
with the doctors, who are dying.

SHIRLEY BREWER (b. 1947)

Alvina and the Bishop

My aunt mixed liquids, counted pills.
From the basement pharmacy,
she sent capsules and elixirs—
small gifts to heal the sick.
Alvina Josephine nurtured patients
she never met, except for the Irish bishop
who asked for her, said:
You put the roses back in my cheeks.
He praised her skills in a verse
she kept next to her rosary.
When Alvina's beloved mother died,
Bishop Kearney offered the mass, his brogue
a salve, a consoling prescription,
a present returned to the sender.

CORTNEY DAVIS (b. 1945)

Stoned

Marion asked for grass. You know, she said. It's true.
It's not the dying, but the pain.
Her friends brought in an ounce,
and when Marion was too weak to roll her little cigarettes,

I'd assign a nurse to help.
One day the supervisor stopped outside the patient's door.
Smell that? she asked
I shook my head.

You must be used to it, she laughed, the smell of death.
Then I could smell it too—
behind the pungent smoke, a scent
slightly off, a little edge to it, like old perfume.

We didn't speak.
Around us, cancer-killing poisons dripped slowly into veins;
everyone was turned and turned again, to keep skin
from breaking down where ribs and bones

poked through, and all the patients' wounds were bound.
Here's what I remember: how Marion laughed
as we nurses with our flimsy cures
pushed every chair against her door

to keep death out. And when we couldn't,
how Marion called me. Hungry. Stoned.

MICHAEL SALCMAN (b. 1946)

The Apprentice Surgeon

"death is the mother of beauty"
             —Wallace Stevens

How awful for him to cut the flesh or watch
a deep cut made before carbolic acid,
before ether, before hope was more than a wretch
on the kerb of the roadside, lungs etched

with cavitation and fawn-colored phlegm.
He knew how death would cork his mouth, killing his speech,
its beauty and necessity. Keats was an apprentice then
to death, his own and all of life beyond its reach:

the nightingale song, the clay of ancient Greece,
and that season of reconciliation for which he longed.
Entombed in life he felt no peace,
despaired of fame and got some of it wrong

while setting some right: dreamed of autumnal skies
while standing at the bedside, attending to the horror at Guy's.

TERESE SVOBODA (b. 1950)

Village Doctor

for Joseph Rocchio, M.D.

Who is closer to the mother
than the doctor at midnight,
who else cares why the infant coughs?
He is husband to the husband,
he is father to all, and none.

Purple shirts, ducktail hair,
as Italian as his shoes,
Doc could finesse any cough:
Put Baby on the phone.
Girls in trouble, troubled

boys—the after after hours
kids—*since we couldn't pay
the doctor, he paid our rent.*
Baby's raisins in the carpet
below the star-framed:
Sorry I kicked you—

don't think your dying
will make us forget.
All we can do, in your life's
midnight, is forgive you
your own damn cough—
you're cured of us.

JOHN STONE (1936–2008)

Getting to Sleep in New Jersey

Not twenty miles from where I work,
William Williams wrote after dark,
after the last baby was caught,
knowing that what he really ought

to do was sleep. Rutherford slept,
while all night William Williams kept

scratching at his prescription pad,
dissecting the good lines from the bad.

He tested the general question whether
feet or butt or head-first ever

determines as well the length of labor
of a poem. His work is over:

bones and guts and red wheelbarrows;
the loneliness and all the errors

a heart can make the other end
of a stethoscope. Outside, the wind

corners the house with a long crow.
Silently, his contagious snow

covers the banks of the Passaic River,
where he walked once, full of fever,

tracking his solitary way
back to his office and the white day,

a peculiar kind of bright-eyed bird,
hungry for morning and the perfect word.

IX.

PATIENTS

CHARLES BAUDELAIRE (1821–1867)

Anywhere Out of This World

This life is a hospital in which each patient is possessed by the desire to change beds. One wants to suffer in front of the stove and another believes that he will get well near the window.

It always seems to me that I will be better off there where I am not, and this question of moving about is one that I discuss endlessly with my soul

Tell me, my soul, my poor chilled soul, what would you think about going to live in Lisbon? It must be warm there, and you'll be able to soak up the sun like a lizard there. That city is on the shore; they say that it is built all out of marble, and that the people there have such a hatred of the vegetable, that they tear down all the trees. There's a country after your own heart—a landscape made out of light and mineral, and liquid to reflect them!

My soul does not reply.

Because you love rest so much, combined with the spectacle of movement, do you want to come and live in Holland, that beatifying land? Perhaps you will be entertained in that country whose image you have so often admired in museums. What do you think of Rotterdam, you who love forests of masts and ships anchored at the foot of houses?

My soul remains mute.

Does Batavia please you more, perhaps? There we would find, after all, the European spirit married to tropical beauty.

Not a word.—Is my soul dead?

Have you then reached such a degree of torpor that you are only happy with your illness? If that's the case, let us flee toward lands that are the analogies of Death.—I've got it, poor soul! We'll pack our bags for Torneo. Let's go even further, to the far end of the Baltic. Even further from life if that is possible: let's go live at the pole. There the sun only grazes the earth obliquely, and the slow alternation of light and darkness suppresses variety and augments monotony, that half of nothingness. There we could take long baths in the shadows, while, to entertain us, the aurora borealis send us from time to time its pink sheaf of sparkling light, like the reflection of fireworks in Hell!

Finally, my soul explodes, and wisely she shrieks at me: IT DOESN'T MATTER WHERE! IT DOESN'T MATTER WHERE! AS LONG AS IT'S OUT OF THIS WORLD!

LINDA PASTAN (b. 1932)

At the Gynecologist's

The body so carefully
contrived for pain,
wakens from the dream of health
again and again
to hands impersonal as wax
and instruments that pry
into the closed chapters of flesh.
See me here, my naked legs
caught in these metal stirrups,
galloping toward death
with flowers of ether in my hair.

Dennis Nurkse (b. 1949)

Things I Forgot to Tell My Doctor

While I waited for you
I peeked at the other patients
—criticizing the girl in headphones
bitterly, for suffering too easily,
intimidated by the old woman with the dog.
When I had given up waiting
I wondered if the nurse liked me
and whether anyone read those magazines
or dusted that potted palm.
I was proud I could read your eye-chart
down to where the letters are symbols,
but leery my mind might impose a pattern.
I made a list of sleepless nights.
Without pride or shame
I longed for what used to be easy:
I can't control my mind
and my body is slipping.
I'm afraid of your small round mirror
that reveals such great distances,
your tongue depressor, your mild music,
and the faith of that stranger
who answers when my name is called.

EDWARD HIRSCH (b. 1950)

Blunt Morning

(July 15, 1979)

I'll never forget that morning when my mother-in-law
floated in a netherworld of morphine-induced sleep,

those lingering hours of an otherwise ordinary Sunday
when she entered into a country that wasn't sleep

so much as a blue comatose state of semi-
consciousness that she inhabited to avoid the pain.

All that blunt sunlit morning we signaled each other
and talked over and around her emaciated shape

propped up on the pillows for what were obviously
her final hours of life on this earth.

She was breathing heavily, she was laboring
in her non-sleep, in her state of drifting

to wherever it was she was going—and suddenly
I couldn't stand it any longer. I moved next to her

and began talking, I didn't ask any questions,
I didn't know what I was saying I was speaking so quickly.

I said that we were all there, all of us, Janet and Sophie
and Susan, who was playing the piano in the living room,

that we loved her intensely, fiercely,
that we missed her *already*—where *was* she?—

we wished we could *do* something, anything,
that we each have tasks to fulfill on this planet

and her job now was to die, which she was doing
so well, so courageously, so gracefully,

we were just amazed at her courage.
I know she could hear me—

and that's when she opened her eyes and fixed me
with her stare. She wasn't moving

but she was looking me precisely in the eyes.
I'll never forget that look—haunted, inquisitive, regal—

and she was speaking,
except her voice was too weak

and the sounds didn't rise beyond her throat,
but she was speaking,

and that's when Janet and Sophie started singing
Hebrew songs—not prayers or psalms but celebratory

songs from Gertrude's childhood in Detroit,
and she was singing, too, she remembered the words,

except we couldn't hear any words, nothing
was coming out of her mouth, but she was tapping

two fingers on the side of the rented hospital bed—
and her lips were moving, she was singing.

That's when Sophie started telling stories
about their childhood, which seemed so far away

and so near, like yesterday, and Gertrude was nodding,
except her head didn't move, but anyone

could see that she was nodding yes,
and then Janet started talking about *her* childhood

in this very room
where sunlight burned through the curtains,

and then suddenly Gertrude jolted forward
and started waving her arms—

What is it? What is it? What is it?—
because she was choking on her own phlegm

and then she fell back against her pillows,
and stopped breathing.

Sylvia Plath (1932–1963)

Face Lift

You bring me good news from the clinic,
Whipping off your silk scarf, exhibiting the tight white
Mummy-cloths, smiling: I'm all right.
When I was nine, a lime-green anesthetist
Fed me banana gas through a frog-mask. The nauseous vault
Boomed with bad dreams and the Jovian voices of surgeons.
The mother swam up, holding a tin basin.
O I was sick.

They've changed all that. Traveling
Nude as Cleopatra in my well-boiled hospital shift,
Fizzy with sedatives and unusually humorous,
I roll to an anteroom where a kind man
Fists my fingers for me. He makes me feel something precious
Is leaking from the finger-vents. At the count of two
Darkness wipes me out like chalk on a blackboard...
I don't know a thing.

For five days I lie in secret,
Tapped like a cask, the years draining into my pillow.
Even my best friend thinks I'm in the country.
Skin doesn't have roots, it peels away easy as paper.
When I grin, the stitches tauten. I grow backward. I'm twenty,
Broody and in long skirts on my first husband's sofa, my fingers
Buried in the lambswool of the dead poodle;
I hadn't a cat yet.

Now she's done for, the dewlapped lady
I watched settle, line by line, in my mirror—
Old sock-face, sagged on a darning egg.
They've trapped her in some laboratory jar.
Let her die there, or whither incessantly for the next fifty years,
Nodding and rocking and fingering her thin hair.
Mother to myself, I wake swaddled in gauze,
Pink and smooth as a baby.

LUCILLE CLIFTON (1936–2010)

Poem to My Uterus

you   uterus
you have been patient
as a sock
while i have slippered into you
my dead and living children
now
they want to cut you out
stocking i will not need
where i am going
where am i going
old girl
without you
uterus
my bloody print
my estrogen kitchen
my black bag of desire
where can i go
barefoot
without you
where can you go
without me

CYNTHIA MARIE HOFFMAN (b. 1975)

Miscarriage

Your baby weighs as much as a paperclip. As an envelope
you forgot to seal the note inside. Your baby is the tip
of an eraser. Your baby is the water spilling past your palm.
The towel came out of the wash like new. The nightgown
you had been wearing came out with all its tiny
purple tulips still blooming. The room is scrubbed
clean as clean can be. Tomorrow, your friend is as far
along as you would be right now. Her baby is a plum.
But for now, your bed is trimmed with the scent of lemons.

KIMBERLY JOHNSON (b. 1971)

Ode On My Episiotomy

Forget pearls, lace-edged kerchiefs, roomy pleats,—
this is my most matronly adornment:
stitches purling up the middle of me
to shut my seam, the one that jagged gaped
upon my fecund, unspeakable dark,
my indecorum needled together
with torquemadan efficiency.
But O! the dream of the dropped stitch! the loophole
through which that unruly within might thread,
catch with a small snag, pull the fray, unknit
the knots unnoticed, and undoily me.

Don't lock up the parlor yet; such pleasure
in unraveling, I may take up the sharps
and darn myself to ladylike again.

DANIEL HOFFMAN (b. 1923–2013)

A Triumph

Himself a doctor, knowing all
the toll, the toll each breath exacts,
breathing faster now because the pain
defines the suffering and the end:
It were best to die
as quickly as a breath is stopt
but he must breathe a thousand breaths,
each breath a dying—

I who was there remember
not so much my mother's anguish
nor the emptiness that fell like blows upon the air,
nor the bewildered whimpering of the children,
but the agony of triumph in resignation blazing
in my grandfather's eyes:
Having tried to die he found
that he who seven hundred times had coursed
harsh air through tiny frightened lungs
could not by force of will surrender
the mortal breath that raged within his own.

ZBIGNIEW HERBERT (1924–1998)

Mr. Cogito Reflects on Suffering

All attempts to avert
the so-called cup of bitterness—
by mental effort
frenzied campaigns on behalf of stray cats
breathing exercises
religion—
let you down

you have to consent
gently bow your head
not wring your hands
use suffering mildly with moderation
like a prosthetic limb
without false shame
but without pride also

don't brandish your stump
over other people's heads
don't knock your white cane
on the panes of the well-fed

drink an extract of bitter herbs
but not to the dregs
be careful to leave
a few gulps for the future

accept it
but at the same time
isolate it in yourself
and if it is possible
make from the stuff of suffering
a thing or a person

play
with it
of course
play

joke around with it
very solicitously
as with a sick child
cajoling in the end
with silly tricks
a wan
smile

DONALD HALL (b. 1928)

Tubes

1
"Up, down, good, bad," said
the man with the tubes
up his nose, "there's lots
of variety . . .
However, notions
of balance between
extremes of fortune
are *stupid*—or at
best unobservant."
He watched as the nurse
fed pellets into
the green nozzle that
stuck from his side. "Mm,"
said the man. "Good. Yum.
(Next time more basil . . .)
When a long-desired
baby is born, what
joy! More happiness
than we find in sex,
more than we take in
success, revenge, or
wealth. But should the same
infant die, would you
measure the horror
on the same rule? Grief
weighs down the seesaw;
joy cannot budge it."

2
"When I was nineteen,
I told a thirty-
year-old man what a
fool I had been when
I was seventeen.

'We were always,' he
said glancing down, 'a
fool two years ago.'"

3
The man with the tubes
up his nostrils spoke
carefully: "I don't
regret what I did,
but that I claimed I
did the opposite.
If I was faithless
or treacherous and
cowardly, I had
my reasons—but I
regret that I called
myself loyal, brave,
and honorable."

4
"Of all illusions,"
said the man with the
tubes up his nostrils,
IVs, catheter,
and feeding nozzle,
"the silliest one
was hardest to lose.
For years I supposed
that after climbing
exhaustedly up
with pitons and ropes,
I would arrive at
last on the plateau
of walking-level-
forever-among-

moss-with-red-blossoms.
But of course, of course:
A continual
climbing is the one
form of arrival
we ever come to—
unless we suppose
that the wished-for height
and house of desire
is tubes up the nose."

RAFAEL CAMPO (b. 1964)

The Distant Moon

I

Admitted to the hospital again.
The second bout of pneumocystis back
In January almost killed him; then,
He'd sworn to us he'd die at home. He baked
Us cookies, which the student wouldn't eat,
Before he left—the kitchen on 5A
Is small, but serviceable and neat.
He told me stories: Richard Gere was gay
And sleeping with a friend of his, and AIDS
Was an elaborate conspiracy
Effected by the government. He stayed
Four months. He lost his sight to CMV.

II

One day, I drew his blood, and while I did
He laughed, and said I was his girlfriend now,
His blood-brother. "Vampire-slut," he cried,
"You'll make me live forever!" Wrinkled brows
Were all I managed in reply. I know
I'm drowning in his blood, his purple blood.
I filled my seven tubes; the warmth was slow
To leave them, pressed inside my palm. I'm sad
Because he doesn't see my face. Because
I can't identify with him. I hate
The fact that he's my age, and that across
My skin he's there, my blood-brother, my mate.

III

He said I was too nice, and after all
If Jodie Foster was a lesbian,
Then doctors could be queer. Residual
Guilts tingled down my spine. "OK, I'm done,"
I said as I withdrew the needle from
His back, and pressed. The CSF was clear;
I never answered him. That spot was framed
In sterile, paper drapes. He was so near
Death, telling him seemed pointless. Then, he died.
Unrecognizable to anyone
But me, he left my needles deep inside
His joking heart. An autopsy was done.

IV

I'd read to him at night. His horoscope,
The New York Times, *The Advocate*;
Some lines by Richard Howard gave us hope.
A quiet hospital is infinite,
The polished, ice-white floors, the darkened halls
That lead to almost anywhere, to death
Or ghostly, lighted Coke machines. I call
To him one night, at home, asleep. His breath,
I dreamed, had filled my lungs—his lips, my lips
Had touched. I felt as though I'd touched a shrine.
Not disrespectfully, but in some lapse
Of concentration. In a mirror shines

The distant moon.

ALICIA SUSKIN OSTRIKER (b. 1937)

from The Mastectomy Poems

THE BRIDGE

You never think it will happen to you,
What happens every day to other women.
Then as you sit paging a magazine,
Its beauties lying idly in your lap,
Waiting to be routinely waved goodbye
Until next year, the mammogram technician
Says *Sorry, we need to do this again,*

And you have already become a statistic,
Citizen of a country where the air,
Water, your estrogen, have just saluted
Their target cells, planted their Judas kiss
Inside the Jerusalem of the breast.
Here on the film what looks like specks of dust
Is calcium deposits.
Go put your clothes on in a shabby booth
Whose curtain reaches halfway to the floor.
Try saying *fear.* Now feel
Your tongue as it cleaves to the roof of your mouth.

Technicalities over, medical articles read,
Decisions made, the Buick's wheels
Nose across Jersey toward the hospital
As if on monorail. Elizabeth
Exhales her poisons, Newark Airport spreads
Her wings—the planes take off over the marsh—
A husband's hand plays with a ring.

Some snowflakes whip across the lanes of cars
Slowed for the tollbooth, and two smoky gulls
Veer by the steel parabolas.
Given a choice of tunnel or bridge
Into Manhattan, the granite crust

On its black platter of rivers, we prefer
Elevation to depth, vista to crawling.

MASTECTOMY

   for Alison Estabrook

I shook your hand before I went.
Your nod was brief, your manner confident,
A ship's captain, and there I lay, a chart
Of the bay, no reefs, no shoals.
While I admired your boyish freckles,
Your soft green cotton gown with the oval neck,
The drug sent me away, like the unemployed.
I swam and supped with the fish, while you
Cut carefully in, I mean
I assume you were careful.
They say it took an hour or so.

I liked your freckled face, your honesty
That first visit, when I said
What's my odds on this biopsy
And you didn't mince words,
One out of four it's cancer.
The degree on your wall shrugged slightly.
Your cold window onto Amsterdam
Had seen everything, bums and operas.
A breast surgeon minces something other
Than language.
That's why I picked you to cut me.

Was I succulent? Was I juicy?
Flesh is grass, yet I dreamed you displayed me
In pleated paper like a candied fruit,
I thought you sliced me like green honeydew

Or like a pomegranate full of seeds
Tart as Persephone's, those electric dots
That kept that girl in hell,
Those jelly pips that made her queen of death.
Doctor, you knifed, chopped and divided it
Like a watermelon's ruby flesh
Flushed a little, serious
About your line of work
Scooped up the risk in the ducts
Scooped up the ducts
Dug out the blubber,
Spooned it off and away, nipple and all.
Eliminated the odds, nipped out
Those almost insignificant cells that might
Or might not have lain dormant forever.

WHAT WAS LOST

What fed my daughters, my son
Trickles of bliss,
My right guess, my true information,
What my husband sucked on
For decades, so that I thought
Myself safe, I thought love
Protected the breast.
What I admired myself, liking
To leave it naked, what I could
Soap and fondle in its bath, what tasted
The drunken airs of summer like a bear
Pawing a hive, half up a sycamore.
I'd let sun eyeball it, surf and lake water
Reel wildly around it, the perfect fit,
The burst of praise. Lifting my chin
I'd stretch my arms to point it at people,
Show it off when I danced. I believed this pride

Would protect it, it was a kind of joke
Between me and my husband
When he licked off some colostrum
Even a drop or two of bitter milk
He'd say *You're saving for your grandchildren.*

I was doing that, and I was saving
The goodness of it for some crucial need,
The way a woman
Undoes her dress to feed
A stranger, at the end of *The Grapes of Wrath*,
A book my mother read me when I was
Spotty with measles, years before
The breast was born, but I remembered it.
How funny I thought goodness would protect it.
Jug of star fluid, breakable cup—

Someone shoveled your good and bad crumbs
Together into a plastic container
Like wet sand at the beach,
For breast tissue is like silicon.
And I imagined inland orange groves,
Each tree standing afire with solid citrus
Lanterns against the gleaming green,
Ready to be harvested and eaten.

WINTERING

> *i had expected more than this.*
> *i had not expected to be*
> *an ordinary woman.*
> —Lucille Clifton

It snows and stops, now it is January,
The houseplants need feeding,

The guests have gone. Today I'm half a boy,
Flat as something innocent, a clean
Plate, just lacking a story.
A woman should be able to say
I've become an Amazon,
Warrior woman minus a breast,
The better to shoot arrow
After fierce arrow,
Or else *I am that dancing Shiva*
Carved in the living rock at Elephanta,
Androgynous deity, but I don't feel
Holy enough or mythic enough.
Taking courage, I told a man *I've resolved*
To be as sexy with one breast
As other people are with two
And he looked away.

Spare me your pity,
Your terror, your condolence.
I'm not your wasting heroine,
Your dying swan. Friend, tragedy
Is a sort of surrender.
Tell me again I'm a model
Of toughness. I eat that up.
I grade papers, I listen to wind,
My husband helps me come, it thaws
A week before semester starts.

Now Schubert plays, and the tenor wheels
Through Heine's lieder. A fifteen-year survivor
Phones: You know what? *You're the same person*
After a mastectomy as before. An idea
That had never occurred to me.
You have a job you like? You have poems to write?
Your marriage is okay? It will stay that way.

The wrinkles are worse. I hate looking in the mirror.
But a missing breast, well, you get used to it.

YEARS OF GIRLHOOD (FOR MY STUDENTS)

All the years of girlhood we wait for them,
Impatient to catch up, to have the power
Inside our sweaters, to replace our mothers.

O full identity, O shape, we figure,
We are God's gift to the world
And the world's gift to God, when we grow breasts,

When the lovers lick them
And bring us there, there, in the fragrant wet,
When the babies nuzzle like bees.

Lucille Clifton (1936–2010)

Lumpectomy Eve

all night i dream of lips
that nursed and nursed
and the lonely nipple

lost in the loss and the need
to feed that turns at last
on itself   that will kill

its body for its hunger's sake
all night i hear the whispering
the soft

      love calls you to this knife
      for love   for love

all night it is the one breast
comforting the other

ROBERT HASS (b. 1941)

A Story About the Body

The young composer, working that summer at an artist's colony, had watched her for a week. She was Japanese, a painter, almost sixty, and he thought he was in love with her. He loved her work, and her work was like the way she moved her body, used her hands, looked at him directly when she mused and considered answers to his questions. One night, walking back from a concert, they came to her door and she turned to him and said, "I think you would like to have me. I would like that too, but I must tell you that I have had a double mastectomy," and when he didn't understand, "I've lost both my breasts." The radiance that he had carried around in his belly and chest cavity—like music— withered quickly, and he made himself look at her when he said, "I'm sorry I don't think I could." He walked back to his own cabin through the pines, and in the morning he found a small blue bowl on the porch outside his door. It looked to be full of rose petals, but he found when he picked it up that the rose petals were on top; the rest of the bowl— she must have swept the corners of her studio—was full of dead bees.

Days of 1994: Alexandrians

for Edmund White

Lunch: as we close the twentieth century,
death, like a hanger-on or a wanna-be
    sits with us at the cluttered bistro
    table, inflecting the conversation.

Elderly friends take lovers, rent studios,
plan trips to unpronounceable provinces.
    Fifty makes the ironic wager
    that his biographer will outlive him—

as may the erudite eighty-one-year-old
dandy with whom a squabble is simmering.
    His green-eyed architect companion
    died in the spring. He is frank about his

grief, as he savors spiced pumpkin soup, and a
sliced rare filet. We'll see the next decade in
    or not. This one retains its flavor.
    "Her new book..." "...brilliant!" "She slept with..." *"Really!"*

Long arabesques of silver-tipped sentences
drift on the current of our two languages
    into the mist of late September
    midafternoon, where the dusk is curling

Just thirty-eight: her last chemotherapy
treatment's the same day classes begin again.
    I went through it a year before she
    started; but hers was both breasts, and lymph nodes.

She's always been a lax vegetarian.
Now she has cut out butter and cheese, and she
never drank wine or beer. What else is
there to eliminate? Tea and coffee . . . ?

(Our avocado salads are copious.)
It's easier to talk about politics
  than to allow the terror that shares
  both of our bedrooms to find words. It made

the introduction; it's an acquaintance we've
in common. Trading medical anecdotes
  helps out when conversation lapses.
  We don't discuss Mitterrand and cancer.

Four months (I say) I'll see her, see him again.
(I dream my life; I wake to contingencies.)
  Now I walk home along the river,
  into the wind, as the clouds break open.

ELIZABETH HARRINGTON (1947–2012)

A Novel Entitled *After the Transplant*

CHAPTER ONE: THE EARLY DAYS

She keeps re-entering that strange state
of Morphine, her body propped up in a hospital bed,
her right hand clasping her left over a crooked
stitched path.

She talks, trudging word by word
through a white landscape.

She gestures but no one notices.

CHAPTER TWO: GETTING IT ALL DOWN

She begins with the story's whole cloth. Then, moving on,
imbues objects with meanings
so odd, they seem suspiciously like displacement.

She pulls metaphor over her as if it were a comforter.

A poem she starts about shoes ends up wandering into the ER.

CHAPTER THREE: MOVING ON

She reads the back of cereal boxes, labels the tops of prescription bottles
with a black felt *Sharpie*, cleans out, against

medical advice, the cat box, watches the Oprah show, wonders
less and less about her donor, whose organ
she wears under rumpled skin, pulsing her own blood, her own DNA.

And she thinks *mine*.
And she thinks *me*.

ELIZABETH ARNOLD (b. 1958)

Heart Valve

They told me there'd be pain

so when I felt it,
sitting at my beat-up farm desk

that looks out glass doors

onto the browning garden—plain sparrows
bathing in the cube-shaped fountain

so violently they drain it,

the white-throats with their
wobbly two-note song

on the long way south still,

and our dogs
out like lights and almost

falling off their chairs

freed of the real-time for awhile
as time began for me

to swell, slow down, carry me out

of all this almost
to a where

about as strong a lure as love.

TED KOOSER (b. 1939)

The Urine Specimen

In the clinic, a sun-bleached shell of stone
on the shore of the city, you enter
the last small chamber, a little closet
chastened with pearl—cool, white, and glistening—
and over the chilly well of the toilet
you trickle your precious sum in a cup.
It's as simple as that. But the heat
of this gold your body's melted and poured out
into a form begins to enthrall you,
warming your hand with your flesh's fevers
in a terrible way. It's like holding
an organ—spleen or fatty pancreas,
a lobe from your foamy brain still steaming
with worry. You know that just outside
a nurse is waiting to cool it into a gel
and slice it onto a microscope slide
for the doctor, who in it will read your future,
wringing his hands. You lift the chalice and toast
the long life of your friend there in the mirror,
who wanly smiles, but does not drink to you.

X.

THE WOUNDED MIND: DEPRESSION & DEMENTIA

JOHN BERRYMAN (1914–1972)

Dream Song No. 67

I don't operate often. When I do,
persons take note.
Nurses look amazed. They pale.
The patient is brought back to life, or so.
The reason I don't do this more (I quote)
is: I have a living to fail—

because of my wife & son—to keep from earning.
—Mr Bones, I sees that.
They for these operations thanks you, what?
not pays you.—Right.
You have seldom been so understanding.
Now there is further a difficulty with the light:

I am obliged to perform in complete darkness
operations of great delicacy
on my self.
—Mr Bones, you terrifies me.
No wonder they didn't pay you. Will you die?
—My
        friend, I succeeded. Later.

T. S. Eliot (1888–1965)

Hysteria

As she laughed I was aware of becoming involved in her laughter
and being part of it, until her teeth were only accidental stars with a
talent for squad-drill. I was drawn in by short gasps, inhaled at each
momentary recovery, lost finally in the dark caverns of her throat,
bruised by the ripple of unseen muscles. An elderly waiter with
trembling hands was hurriedly spreading a pink and white checked
cloth over the rusty green iron table, saying: "If the lady and gentleman
wish to take their tea in the garden, if the lady and gentleman wish
to take their tea in the garden . . . " I decided that if the shaking of her
breasts could be stopped, some of the fragments of the afternoon might
be collected, and I concentrated my attention with careful subtlety to
this end.

WELDON KEES (1914–1955)

Aspects of Robinson

Robinson at cards at the Algonquin; a thin
Blue light comes down once more outside the blinds.
Gray men in overcoats are ghosts blown past the door.
The taxis streak the avenues with yellow, orange, and red.
This is Grand Central, Mr. Robinson.

Robinson on a roof above the Heights; the boats
Mourn like the lost. Water is slate, far down.
Through sounds of ice cubes dropped in glass, an osteopath,
Dressed for the links, describes an old Intourist tour.
—Here's where old Gibbons jumped from, Robinson.

Robinson walking in the Park, admiring the elephant.
Robinson buying the *Tribune*, Robinson buying the *Times*. Robinson
Saying, "Hello. Yes, this is Robinson. Sunday
At five? I'd love to. Pretty well. And you?"
Robinson alone at Longchamps, staring at the wall.

Robinson afraid, drunk, sobbing Robinson
In bed with a Mrs. Morse. Robinson at home;
Decisions: Toynbee or luminol? Where the sun
Shines, Robinson in flowered trunks, eyes toward
The breakers. Where the night ends, Robinson in East Side bars.

Robinson in Glen plaid jacket, Scotch-grain shoes,
Black four-in-hand and oxford button-down,
The jeweled and silent watch that winds itself, the brief-
Case, covert topcoat, clothes for spring, all covering
His sad and usual heart, dry as a winter leaf.

DONALD JUSTICE (1925–2004)

Counting the Mad

This one was put in a jacket,
This one was sent home,
This one was given bread and meat
But would eat none,
And this one cried No No No No
All day long.

This one looked at the window
As though it were a wall,
This one saw things that were not there,
And this one cried No No No No
All day long.

This one thought himself a bird,
This one a dog,
And this one thought himself a man,
An ordinary man,
And cried and cried No No No No
All day long.

ROBERT PINSKY (b. 1940)

from Essay on Psychiatrists

INVOCATION

It's crazy to think one could describe them—
Calling on reason, fantasy, memory, eyes and ears—
As though they were all alike any more

Than sweeps, opticians, poets or masseurs.
Moreover, they are for more than one reason
Difficult to speak of seriously and freely,

And I have never (even this is difficult to say
Plainly, without foolishness or irony)
Consulted one for professional help, though it happens

Many or most of my friends have—and that,
Perhaps, is why it seems urgent to try to speak
Sensibly about them, about the psychiatrists.

SOME TERMS

"Shrink" is a misnomer. The religious
Analogy is all wrong, too, and the old,
Half-forgotten jokes about Viennese accents

And beards hardly apply to the good-looking woman
In boots and a knit dress, or the man
Seen buying the Sunday *Times* in mutton-chop

Whiskers and expensive running shoes.
In a way I suspect that even the terms "doctor"
And "therapist" are misnomers; the patient

Is not necessarily "sick." And one assumes
That no small part of the psychiatrist's
Role is just that: to point out misnomers.

THEIR SPEECH, COMPARED WITH WISDOM AND POETRY

Terms of all kinds mellow with time, growing
Arbitrary and rich as we call this man "neurotic"
Or that man "a peacock." The lore of psychiatrists—

"Paranoid," "Anal" and so on, if they still use
Such terms—also passes into the status of old sayings:
Water thinner than blood or under bridges; bridges

Crossed in the future or burnt in the past. Or the terms
Of myth, the phrases that well up in my mind:
Two blind women and a blind little boy, running—

Easier to cut thin air into planks with a saw
And then drive nails into those planks of air,
Than to evade those three, the blind harriers,

The tireless blind women and the blind boy, pursuing
For long years of my life, for long centuries of time.
Concerning Justice, Fortune and Love I believe

That there may be wisdom, but no science and few terms:
Blind, and blinding, too. Hot in pursuit and flight,
Justice, Fortune and Love demand the arts

Of knowing and naming: and, yes, the psychiatrists, too,
Patiently naming them. But all in pursuit and flight, two
Blind women, tireless, and the blind little boy.

ANNE SEXTON (1928–1974)

from The Double Image

I am thirty this November.
You are still small, in your fourth year.
We stand watching the yellow leaves go queer,
flapping in the winter rain,
falling flat and washed. And I remember
mostly the three autumns you did not live here.
They said I'd never get you back again.
I tell you what you'll never really know:
all the medical hypothesis
that explained my brain will never be as true as these
struck leaves letting go.

I, who chose two times
to kill myself, had said your nickname
the mewling months when you first came;
until a fever rattled
in your throat and I moved like a pantomime
above your head. Ugly angels spoke to me. The blame,
I heard them say, was mine. They tattled
like green witches in my head, letting doom
leak like a broken faucet;
as if doom had flooded my belly and filled your bassinet,
an old debt I must assume.

Death was simpler than I'd thought.
The day life made you well and whole
I let the witches take away my guilty soul.
I pretended I was dead
until the white men pumped the poison out,
putting me armless and washed through the rigamarole
of talking boxes and the electric bed.
I laughed to see the private iron in that hotel.
Today the yellow leaves
go queer. You ask me where they go. I say today believed
in itself, or else it fell.

Today, my small child, Joyce,
love your self's self where it lives.
There is no special God to refer to; or if there is,
why did I let you grow
in another place. You did not know my voice
when I came back to call. All the superlatives
of tomorrow's white tree and mistletoe
will not help you know the holidays you had to miss.
The time I did not love
myself, I visited your shoveled walks; you held my glove.
There was new snow after this.

*

They sent me letters with news
of you and I made moccasins that I would never use.
When I grew well enough to tolerate
myself, I lived with my mother. Too late,
too late, to live with your mother, the witches said.
But I didn't leave. I had my portrait
done instead.

Part way back from Bedlam
I came to my mother's house in Gloucester,
Massachusetts. And this is how I came
to catch at her; and this is how I lost her.
I cannot forgive your suicide, my mother said.
And she never could. She had my portrait
done instead.

I lived like an angry guest,
like a partly mended thing, an outgrown child.
I remember my mother did her best.
She took me to Boston and had my hair restyled.
Your smile is like your mother's, the artist said.

I didn't seem to care. I had my portrait
done instead.

There was a church where I grew up
with its white cupboards where they locked us up,
row by row, like puritans or shipmates
singing together. My father passed the plate.
Too late to be forgiven now, the witches said.
I wasn't exactly forgiven. They had my portrait
done instead.

*

I checked out for the last time
on the first of May;
graduate of the mental cases,
with my analyst's okay,
my complete book of rhymes,
my typewriter and my suitcases.

All that summer I learned life
back into my own
seven rooms, visited the swan boats,
the market, answered the phone,
served cocktails as a wife
should, made love among my petticoats

and August tan. And you came each
weekend. But I lie.
You seldom came. I just pretended
you, small piglet, butterfly
girl with jelly bean cheeks,
disobedient three, my splendid

stranger. And I had to learn
why I would rather
die than love, how your innocence
would hurt and how I gather
guilt like a young intern
his symptoms, his certain evidence.

That October day we went
to Gloucester the red hills
reminded me of the dry red fur fox
coat I played in as a child; stock-still
like a bear or a tent,
like a great cave laughing or a red fur fox.

We drove past the hatchery,
the hut that sells bait,
past Pigeon Cove, past the Yacht Club, past Squall's
Hill, to the house that waits
still, on the top of the sea,
and two portraits hung on the opposite walls.

*

I could not get you back
except for weekends. You came
each time, clutching the picture of a rabbit
that I had sent you. For the last time I unpack
your things. We touch from habit.
The first visit you asked my name.
Now you stay for good. I will forget
how we bumped away from each other like marionettes
on strings. It wasn't the same
as love, letting weekends contain
us. You scrape your knee. You learn my name,
wobbling up the sidewalk, calling and crying.

You call me *mother* and I remember my mother again,
somewhere in greater Boston, dying.

I remember we named you Joyce
so we could call you Joy.
You came like an awkward guest
that first time, all wrapped and moist
and strange at my heavy breast.
I needed you. I didn't want a boy,
only a girl, a small milky mouse
of a girl, already loved, already loud in the house
of herself. We named you Joy.
I, who was never quite sure
about being a girl, needed another
life, another image to remind me.
And this was my worst guilt; you could not cure
nor soothe it. I made you to find me.

JOHN BRICUTH (b. 1940)

Song: Hypochondria As the Basis for Conversion

Fallen on the time
When the pulse less steady
Starts the darkening mind
Musing on the body,
Every catch in the breath
Is the sickness unto death.

The back's real ache,
The eye's fictitious twitch,
The existential quake,
The sympathetic itch
Find their way to the head,
Bare the concept of dread.

What if minds crude
As sick-call in the service
Know no attitude
Between the dead and nervous,
Nor that body's made for
The spirit's stiff either/or?

True hypochondriacs,
Treading psychic nettles,
Sit on neural tacks,
Lie on moral needles,
Know body's ills are soul dissembling,
Fever and chills, fear and trembling.

Consciousness of self
Is that anguished gain
More valuable than health.
If imagined pain
Is what it takes to bring us to,
Then seize the dying point of view.

We're dying, doctor, dying
A fragment of a life,
And your sterile lying
And your clinic laugh
Cannot void the pen dipped
For the unscientific postscript.

DICK ALLEN (b. 1939)

Agoraphobic

Fear makes him afraid, the sudden awareness
    of the sky's empty height,
his dizzying perception of a crowded room
    where strangers might come up to him at any moment;
at any moment he might faint. The inner seats
    of movie houses; lines
which move too slowly toward the cashier's cage,
    the endless lines. The endless empty talk
he can neither focus nor escape—his face
    flushed suddenly, his mind
searching for a steady thought, some bright
    spot of interest in the tangled stream
of voices, faces, lights
    which seek him out. How did
he function, unafraid? What kept him from
    seeing that the doors were shut, the windows closed,
the meeting could last hours with no pause?
    What kind of fool could sit there comfortably
and not think I am dying, there's no time
    to waste? What fool
could ride a boat three hours off the Keys
    to visit coral reefs, or wake
up eager to be anywhere but in
    a pleasant house? *I am*
ashamed, he thinks, for all those years
    I spent as if the sky could never fall,
I lived close neighbors with the death
    of all—and did not notice how a room
can spin off axis, hands can slip
    from mine and not return, how everything
is but vibrating space, and has
    no meaning given but the one I take
from fear that at the last I will not break
    but dissolve, dissolve.

RACHEL HADAS (b. 1948)

The Hotel

Living with dementia is like riding on a carousel.
I said dementia is like a big old carousel.
And you can't get off, but it turns into a hotel.

Year after year they reserve you the same space.
Year after year they save you the same old place.
They forget your name, but they never forget a face.

Who's going to visit you? Don't expect your friends.
No use getting up for visits from your friends.
It goes on this way and who knows how it ends?

Well, you sit there, baby, and you don't say a word.
Yup, there you sit, not saying a single word.
Or if you did, I guess I never heard.

Sometimes I wonder what's going through your head.
Yes, who knows what is cooking in your head?
No one gets to look in there till you are dead.

I'd like to cry, but I have no more tears.
I said I'm done crying, I've run out of tears.
Before and now and after, years and years.

Vijay Seshadri (b. 1954)

Nursing Home

1.

She had dreams fifty years ago
she remembers on this day.
She dreamed about Bombay.
It looked like Rio.
She dreamed about Rio,

which looked like itself, though
Rio was a city she'd never seen—
not on TV, not in a magazine.
Brain scans done on her show

her perisylvian pathways and declivities
choked by cities,
microscopic mercurial cities
made from her memories,

good and bad,
from the things she saw but didn't see,
from the remembered pressure
of every lover she ever had.

2.

Unexpected useful combinations between cognitive psychology
and neuroscience have fostered new observational protocols not
only for elderly patients in the Lewy body pathologic subgroup but
those discovered across a wide spectrum of dementias and dementia-
induced phenomena, including but not limited to Normal Pressure
Hydrocephalus (NPH), classical Alzheimer's disease (AD), and the
deformations in mental recognition and function (*Dear, eat the soup
with the spoon, not the fork*), the coruscating visions (*Who is that laid out
in my bed?*), the spontaneous motor features of Parkinsonism. Synaptic
patterns embodied in sparks, showers, electrical cascades, waterfalls,
and shooting stars are increasingly revealing an etiology proximately to
be fully established and suggestive links between processes strictly

biochemical and ideational and linguistic explosions for which documentation has been massive while analysis has, so far, been scant. While an adequate conceptual apparatus still remains out of reach, progress across a broad frontier of research has been sufficiently dramatic to suggest possible developments that will lead both to therapeutic remedies for distressed elderly patients and to a synthesis among various disciplines that have heretofore seemed not just incompatible but in direct conflict with one another. Certain coherencies have been unearthed that have truly startled our consensus . . .

3.
—She doesn't know any better than to act the fool.

—Is she dead? No, she's not dead.

—Is she dead?

—No, I'm not dead, and I don't want anybody to think I'm dead.

—Do you think it's funny?

—Wonder why she acts like that?

—Is she dead? No, she's not dead, and I'm not dead, neither.

—Is she really dead? No, she's not dead, but she's acting the fool.

—Are you really dead? No, I'm not really dead. I'm just acting the fool

—I'll show you how I can act the fool.

—No, I don't think I look nice. I think I look purty.

—No, I'm not dead. I just act like I'm dead.

—What makes you want to act like she's dead?

—Do you think she's dead?

—Do you think she's dead, or is she just acting the fool?

C. K. WILLIAMS (b. 1936)

Alzheimer's: The Wife

She answers the bothersome telephone, takes the message, forgets the
    message, forgets who called.
One of their daughters, her husband guesses: the one with the dogs, the
    babies, the boy Jed?
Yes, perhaps, but how tell which, how tell anything when all the name
    tags have been lost or switched,
when all the lonely flowers of sense and memory bloom and die now in
    adjacent bites of time?
Sometimes her own face will suddenly appear with terrifying
    inappropriateness before her in a mirror.
She knows that if she's patient, its gaze will break, demurely,
    decorously, like a well-taught child's,
it will turn from her as though it were embarrassed by the secrets of
    this awful hide-and-seek.
If she forgets, though, and glances back again, it will still be in there,
    furtively watching, crying.

RACHEL HADAS (b. 1948)

The Boat

All day I bustle in and out
While you're at home. No, far away.
All night we sail in the same boat.

I think of trying to invite
Friends whom we no longer see.
All day I'm busy—in and out.

For you the hours accumulate
Or fly by, maybe—don't ask me.
At night we sail in the same boat.

The ties that bind have grown too tight.
Entangled, you sit peacefully;
I squirm and struggle to get out.

Angry, impatient, or contrite,
I stir the pot of poetry.
At night we idle in our boat.

To lose a self without a fight...
You barely have a word to say.
My mind's revolving, in and out.
Nights we sail blindly in our boat.

JOHN BERRYMAN (1914–1972)

Dream Song No. 235

Tears Henry shed for poor old Hemingway
Hemingway in despair, Hemingway at the end,
the end of Hemingway,
tears in a diningroom in Indiana
and that was years ago, before his marriage say,
God to him no worse luck send.

Save us from shotguns & fathers' suicides.
It all depends on who you're the father *of*
if you want to kill yourself—
a bad example, murder of oneself,
the final death, in a paroxysm, of love
for which good mercy hides?

A girl at the door: 'A few coppers pray'
But to return, to return to Hemingway
that cruel and gifted man.
Mercy! my father; do not pull the trigger
or all my life I'll suffer from your anger
killing what you began.

D. H. LAWRENCE (1885–1930)

Sick

I am sick, because I have given myself away.
I have given myself to the people when they came
so cultured, even bringing little gifts,
so they pecked a shred of my life, and flew off with a croak
of sneaking exultance.
So now I have lost too much, and am sick.

I am trying now to learn never
to give of my life to the dead,
never, not the tiniest shred.

XI.

THE FINAL JOURNEY: DEATH & DYING

WILLIAM SHAKESPEARE (1564–1616)

That time of year thou mayst in me behold

That time of year thou mayst in me behold
When yellow leaves, or none, or few, do hang
Upon those boughs which shake against the cold,
Bare ruined choirs, where late the sweet birds sang.
In me thou seest the twilight of such day
As after sunset fadeth in the west,
Which by and by black night doth take away,
Death's second self, that seals up all in rest.
In me thou seest the glowing of such fire
That on the ashes of his youth doth lie
As the death-bed whereon it must expire
Consumed with that which it was nourished by.
    This thou perceiv'st, which makes thy love more strong,
    To love that well which thou must leave ere long.

EMILY DICKINSON (1830–1836)

After Great Pain, a Formal Feeling Comes

After great pain, a formal feeling comes—
The Nerves sit ceremonious, like Tombs—
The stiff Heart questions 'was it He, that bore,'
And Yesterday, or Centuries before'?

The Feet, mechanical, go round—
A Wooden way
Of Ground, or Air, or Ought—
Regardless grown,
A Quartz contentment, like a stone—

This is the Hour of Lead—
Remembered, if outlived,
As Freezing persons, recollect the Snow—
First—Chill—then Stupor—then the letting go—

William Carlos Williams (1883–1963)

The Last Words of My English Grandmother

There were some dirty plates
and a glass of milk
beside her on a small table
near the rank, disheveled bed—

Wrinkled and nearly blind
she lay and snored
rousing with anger in her tones
to cry for food,

Gimme something to eat—
They're starving me—
I'm all right I won't go
to the hospital. No, no, no

Give me something to eat
Let me take you
to the hospital, I said
and after you are well

you can do as you please.
She smiled, Yes
you do what you please first
then I can do what I please—

Oh, oh, oh! she cried
as the ambulance men lifted
her to the stretcher—
Is this what you call

making me comfortable?
By now her mind was clear—
Oh you think you're smart
you young people,

she said, but I'll tell you
you don't know anything.
Then we started.
On the way

we passed a long row
of elms. She looked at them
awhile out of
the ambulance window and said,

What are all those
fuzzy-looking things out there?
Trees? Well, I'm tired
of them and rolled her head away.

JOHN DONNE (1572–1631)

Hymn to God my God, In My Sickness

Since I am coming to that holy room,
    Where, with Thy choir of saints for evermore,
I shall be made Thy music, as I come
    I tune the instrument here at the door,
    And what I must do then, think here before.

Whil'st my physicians by their love are grown
    Cosmographers, and I their map, who lie
Flat on this bed, that by them may be shown
    That this is my South-west discovery
    Per fretum febris, by these straits to die.

I joy, that in these straits I see my West;
    For, though their currents yield return to none,
What shall my West hurt me ? As West and East
    In all flat maps (and I am one) are one,
    So death doth touch the resurrection.

Is the Pacific Sea my home? Or are
    The Eastern riches? Is Jerusalem?
Anyan, and Magellan, and Gibraltar.
    All straits, and none but straits, are ways to them,
    Whether where Japhet dwelt, or Cham, or Shem.

We think that paradise and calvary,
    Christ's cross and Adam's tree, stood in one place;
Look, Lord, and find both Adams met in me;
    As the first Adam's sweat surrounds my face,
    May the last Adam's blood my soul embrace.

So, in His purple wrapped, receive me Lord,
    By these his Thorns, give me, his other crown;
And as to others' souls I preached Thy word,
    Be this my text, my sermon to mine own,
Therefore that He may raise the Lord throws down.

PHILIP LARKIN (1922–1985)

Heads in the Women's Ward

On pillow after pillow lies
The wild white hair and staring eyes;
Jaws stand open; necks are stretched
With every tendon sharply sketched;
A bearded mouth talks silently
To someone no one else can see.

Sixty years ago they smiled
At lover, husband, first-born child.

Smiles are for youth. For old age come
Death's terror and delirium.

MICHAEL RYAN (b. 1946)

A Good Father

The cancer's eaten half his liver.
The bile's going to the brain.
With one night more at most to live,
he's acting insane.

The food his family brings is poison.
Not one of them has ever cared.
What a life he would have lived without them,
if only he'd dared.

Conversations while he's sleeping—
in the hallway, on the phone—
link his dear ones in forgiveness
while he alone

joins the torments of resentment
swelling to its highest power
that will take him like a whirlwind
across the river of fire.

Robert Pinsky (b. 1940)

Dying

Nothing to be said about it, and everything—
The change of changes, closer or further away:
The Golden Retriever next door, Gussie, is dead,

Like Sandy, the Cocker Spaniel from three doors down
Who died when I was small; and every day
Things that were in my memory fade and die.

Phrases die out: first, everyone forgets
What doornails are; then after certain decades
As a dead metaphor, *"dead as a doornail"* flickers

And fades away. But someone I know is dying–
And though one might say glibly, "everyone is,"
The different pace make the difference absolute.

The tiny invisible spores in the air we breathe,
That settle harmlessly on our drinking water
And on our skin, happen to come together

With certain conditions on the forest floor,
Or even a shady corner of the lawn–
And overnight the fleshy, pale stalks gather,

The colorless growth without a leaf or flower;
And around the stalks, the summer grass keeps growing
With steady pressure, like the insistent whiskers

That grow between shaves on a face, the nails
Growing and dying from the toes and fingers
At their own humble pace, oblivious

As the nerveless moths, that live their night or two—
Though like a moth a bright soul keeps on beating,
Bored and impatient in the monster's mouth.

ELIZABETH HARRINGTON (1947–2012)

Sending My Mother Home After My Surgery

My mother dreams of white horses
        with red-tinted ornaments in their manes.
                She can't make them stop,

she says, she can't sleep, for the sake of the horses.
Should she leave me? Is it safe?
        I know she's thinking

of her too quiet apartment, the pinch of dark, falling
from her four poster bed;
                but not death, she says, it's not death

that worries her. There are worse things,
        like being forgotten, smiled over
                by strangers, smug and indifferent

in the event she becomes dependent
        and moved to a nursing home which, she says,
                would be worse than death

and don't think she doesn't mean it
        and I know, I do know
                I tell her as I did when my sister and I

stood in the street with her once and told her we
        would never do that,
                before she could be coaxed

back in the front seat of the car where she sat silent
        all the way home, staring out the window
                at nothing I could see.

MARIE HOWE (b. 1950)

Pain

He rose on the surface of it like the layer of water on top of a wave
that won't break—you've seen those swells—

cold and moving like something breathing you can't see, collecting and
collecting until it seems uncontainable, heaving on and on, rising and

rising and growing bigger.
When it got very bad, he'd say, Tell me a story,

and after an hour or so, he'd say, We got through that one, didn't we?

Until a day came when he said, Marie,
you know how we've been waiting for the big pain to come?

I think it's here. I think this is it.
I think it's been here all along.

And he did take the morphine, and he died the next week.

JASON SHINDER (1955–2008)

Ocean

Goodbye again. Say there is a little song in my head

And because of it I can't sleep or change my mind
about the future. Now the song runs all the way down

to the beach where I sit as if the sky

were my room now. No one, not even you,
can hear me singing. Not even me.

As if the music rose from the mouth of the ocean.

No mouth. Like rain before it reaches us.
Like wind twirling dresses on the clothesline.

Who has no one has the history of the ocean.

Lord, give me two more days. So that
the last moments may be with someone.

Tony Hoagland (b. 1953)

Lucky

If you are lucky in this life,
you will get to help your enemy
the way I got to help my mother
when she was weakened past the point of saying no.

Into the big enamel tub
half-filled with water
which I had made just right,
I lowered the childish skeleton
she had become.

Her eyelids fluttered as I soaped and rinsed
her belly and her chest,
the sorry ruin of her flanks
and the frayed gray cloud
between her legs.

Some nights, sitting by her bed
book open in my lap
while I listened to the air
move thickly in and out of her dark lungs,
my mind filled up with praise
as lush as music,

amazed at the symmetry and luck
that would offer me the chance to pay
my heavy debt of punishment and love
with love and punishment.

And once I held her dripping wet
in the uncomfortable air
between the wheelchair and the tub,
and she begged me like a child

to stop,
an act of cruelty which we both understood
was the ancient irresistible rejoicing
of power over weakness.

If you are lucky in this life,
you will get to raise the spoon
of pristine, frosty ice cream
to the trusting creature mouth
of your old enemy

because the tastebuds at least are not broken
because there is a bond between you
and sweet is sweet in any language.

Rosanna Warren (b. 1953)

Aftermath

"Dawn. The moment it was
it was over."
                    —Deborah Tall

It was that last, euphoric summer, between
one chemo and another, when you looked out
your kitchen window and saw the doe standing
at the edge of your lawn where the thicket gathers—
autumn olive, buckthorn, forsythia, dogwood.
And when you stepped outside, the doe stayed still
and looked in your eyes, you thought, with a companionable
complicit question, and didn't run. You were
light-headed. The doe lowered her nose
to shove at the small bundle at her feet
folded up like an awkward deck chair
till then invisible in its hollow of grass.
She had just given birth. The fawn couldn't stand
but raised its too-large head to gaze at you.
You were, as you said, already more or less
posthumous. You took each other in.
One of you before, the other beyond fear.
Two creatures, side effects on one another,
headed in opposite directions.

Thomas Nashe (1567–c.1601)

A Litany in Time of Plague

from Summer's Last Will and Testament

Adieu, farewell, earth's bliss;
This world uncertain is;
Fond are life's lustful joys;
Death proves them all but toys;
None from his darts can fly;
I am sick, I must die.
Lord, have mercy on us!

Rich men, trust not in wealth,
Gold cannot buy you health;
Physic himself must fade.
All things to end are made,
The plague full swift goes by;
I am sick, I must die.
Lord, have mercy on us!

Beauty is but a flower
Which wrinkles will devour;
Brightness falls from the air;
Queens have died young and fair;
Dust hath closed Helen's eye.
I am sick, I must die.
Lord, have mercy on us!

Strength stoops unto the grave,
Worms feed on Hector brave;
Swords may not fight with fate,
Earth still holds open her gate.
"Come, come!" the bells do cry.
I am sick, I must die.
Lord, have mercy on us!

Wit with his wantonness
Tasteth death's bitterness;
Hell's executioner
Hath no ears for to hear
What vain art can reply.
I am sick, I must die.
      Lord, have mercy on us!

JASON SHINDER (1955–2008)

Arrow Breaking Apart

While lovers sleep, I dig my nails into the earth,

holding up traffic. Just now a cloud has pulled up
while I was talking to the Emptiness

of the Universe and my voice plugged into the waves

at the bottom of the ocean.
My heart is taped up like a child's drawing

of the moon over the broken window of the sky

where the wind always comes back to fill my lungs.
I will dance on my shadow. I will open my mouth

with the air inside my mother's coffin.

I will be the arrow breaking apart in the body
of the blackbird, which appears at my window, singing.

JANE KENYON (1947–1995)

Otherwise

I got out of bed
on two strong legs.
It might have been
otherwise. I ate
cereal, sweet
milk, ripe, flawless
peach. It might
have been otherwise.
I took the dog uphill
to the birch wood.
All morning I did
the work I love.

At noon I lay down
with my mate. It might
have been otherwise.
We ate dinner together
at a table with silver
candlesticks. It might
have been otherwise.
I slept in a bed
in a room with paintings
on the walls, and
planned another day
just like this day.
But one day, I know,
it will be otherwise.

JOHN DONNE (1572–1631)

Holy Sonnet No. 10

Death, be not proud, though some have called thee
   Mighty and dreadful, for thou art not so.
   For those, whom thou think'st thou dost overthrow
Die not, poor Death, nor yet canst thou kill me.
From rest and sleep, which but thy pictures be,
   Much pleasure; then, from thee, much more must flow,
   And soonest our best men with thee do go,
Rest of their bones, and soul's delivery.
Thou'rt slave to fate, chance, kings, and desperate men,
   And dost with poison, war, and sickness dwell,
   And poppy, or charms can make us sleep as well,
And better than thy stroke. Why swell'st thou then?
   One short sleep past, we live eternally,
   And Death shall be no more. Death, thou shalt die.

XII.

The View from the Other Side of the Bed: Loved Ones of the Sick

C. P. Cavafy (1863–1933)

Body, Remember

Body, remember not only how much you were loved,
not only the beds you lay on,
but also those desires that glowed openly
in eyes that looked at you,
trembled for you in the voices—
only some chance obstacle frustrated them.
Now that it's all finally in the past,
it seems almost as if you gave yourself
to those desires too—how they glowed,
remember, in eyes that looked at you,
remember, body, how they trembled for you in those voices.

Florence Weinberger (b. 1932)

Getting in Bed with a Man Who Is Sick

Every night I get in bed with a man who is sick.
I have to move fluidly and stiffly,
as if a healthy thrust
under the blankets, a shift
of my body to find the right spot
could cause his body to end up in agony.
All through the night, in my sleep,
I hear his moans,
constant now as breathing.
His flesh is disappearing.
More and more I see his bones. In some places
I see right through his skin
to the blue-pebbled tumors
erupting there, pushing in two ways,
toward the light and toward the death
of their unwilling host.
His breathing is labored. His voice
has changed. Tonight
he kissed me back brief and hard with a strength
I thought I'd never know from him again.
See, it said, I remember. I wonder
if that will become one of those moments
we tend not to forget; that come to be
all of it together, so we can say it
sometime in the future
in one sentence
and don't have to replay the life and the dying over
and over again. When we are sleeping
alone, and we wake, and the walls are breathing,
and they are the company we keep.

WILLIAM CARLOS WILLIAMS (1883–1963)

The Widow's Lament In Springtime

Sorrow is my own yard
where the new grass
flames as it has flamed
often before but not
with the cold fire
that closes round me this year.
Thirtyfive years
I lived with my husband.
The plumtree is white today
with masses of flowers.
Masses of flowers
load the cherry branches
and color some bushes
yellow and some red
but the grief in my heart
is stronger than they
for though they were my joy
formerly, today I notice them
and turned away forgetting.
Today my son told me
that in the meadows,
at the edge of the heavy woods
in the distance, he saw
trees of white flowers.
I feel that I would like
to go there
and fall into those flowers
and sink into the marsh near them.

WELDON KEES (1914–1955)

The Doctor Will Return

The surgical mask, the rubber teat
Are singed, give off an evil smell.
You seem to weep more now that heat
Spreads everywhere we look.
It says here none of us is well.

The warty spottings on the figurines
Are nothing you would care to claim.
You seem to weep more since the magazines
Began revivals on the Dundas book.
It says here you were most to blame.

But though I cannot believe that this is so,
I mark the doctor as a decent sort.
I mix your medicine and go
Downstairs to leave instructions for the cook.
It says here time is getting short.

That I can believe. I hear you crying in your room
While watching traffic, reconciled.
Out in the park, black flowers are in bloom.
I picked some once and pressed them in a book.
You used to look at them, and smile.

HARVEY SHAPIRO (1924–2013)

6/20/97

It's Friday night and I've just had
another helping of Ben and Jerry's coffee
fudge frozen yogurt because I saw
David Ignatow at Columbia Presbyterian,
8th floor, Milstein, room 426, after a quick
ride on the skip 9, the one that does
every other stop, and David, who is
recovering from a stroke, doesn't look
too good, a transparent mask over
his face, feeding him oxygen, whiffs of
steam eddying from it, or maybe con-
trails because David is going very fast,
talking to himself and jerking his body
violently. On the other hand, the view
from his window is splendid, the
lordly Hudson cloaked in late afternoon
sun. I say to the nurse, his color is good,
and she says, that's because we're giving
him blood, pointing to the tubing. Count
Dracula was right, she says, it
makes you look good.
But it's not for real.

GORDON GRIGSBY (b. 1927)

Dying Together

Paralyzed and awake
like prey stung by a wasp
she lies like a stranger in her own body
in a bed in the old dining room.
At times her eyes open, glazed, and stare
but her mind works always, clear and sharp as a watch
talking to her, talking to her—
'It's not much to ask,
   to die in your house"
—knowing the fibers will sometime twitch
in his heart, his mind blacken, his tissues fail
to lift her in her need,
both of them sprawl on the floor, one dying, one dead,
like grotesque lovers, spent, the house cold,
the phone out of reach, her mind working like a watch.

And he, caught in a line
in the supermarket, delaying, prolonging
this little freedom, nursing his time
among strangers, he stares
with odd intentness down
at the small heap of food in the cart,
a single package with blood in its corners,
and thinks—"If I could only get her to eat."

He moves a few feet toward a friend, the cashier,
and it suddenly happens then that he knows
fifty years' love
   seeping like blood
through stunned membranes into his lungs
and, shielding his eyes, he waits
with shorter and shorter breaths,
as if he can't help it, waits
paralyzed and awake.

DONALD HALL (b. 1928)

The Ship Pounding

Each morning I made my way
among gangways, elevators,
and nurses' pods to Jane's room
to interrogate the grave helpers
who tended her through the night
while the ship's massive engines
kept its propellers turning.
Week after week, I sat by her bed
with black coffee and the *Globe*.
The passengers on this voyage
wore masks or cannulae
or dangled devices that dripped
chemicals into their wrists.
I believed that the ship
traveled to a harbor
of breakfast, work, and love.
I wrote: "When the infusions
are infused entirely, bone
marrow restored and lymphoblasts
remitted, I will take my wife,
bald as Michael Jordan,
back to our dog and day." Today,
months later at home, these
words turned up on my desk
as I listened in case Jane called
for help, or spoke in delirium,
ready to make the agitated
drive to Emergency again
for readmission to the huge
vessel that heaves water month
after month, without leaving
port, without moving a knot,
without arrival or destination,
its great engines pounding.

ALICIA OSTRIKER (b. 1937)

Lymphoma

I come from visiting my once-blonde
friend in hospital with non-Hodgkin's
lymphoma the chemo is working

we chat about other women's husbands
suffering from Parkinson's
we laugh cry hug we feel a little lucky

down the hall an attendant rolls a gurney
yellowish old man skull glares
from under a blanket

now how in hell do I get out
can't find elevator or stairs
despite red neon EXIT signs everywhere

SEAMUS HEANEY (1939–2013)

Mid-Term Break

I sat all morning in the college sick bay
Counting bells knelling classes to a close.
At two o'clock our neighbors drove me home.

In the porch I met my father crying-
He had always taken funerals in his stride-
And Big Jim Evans saying it was a hard blow.

The baby cooed and laughed and rocked the pram
When I came in, and I was embarrassed
By old men standing up to shake my hand

And tell me they were 'sorry for my trouble'.
Whispers informed strangers I was the eldest,
Away at school, as my mother held my hand

In hers and coughed out angry tearless sighs.
At ten o'clock the ambulance arrived
With the corpse, stanched and bandaged by the nurses.

Next morning I went up into the room. Snowdrops
And candles soothed the bedside; I saw him
For the first time in six weeks. Paler now,

Wearing a poppy bruise on his left temple,
He lay in the four foot box as in his cot.
No gaudy scars, the bumper knocked him clear.

A four foot box, a foot for every year.

ALFRED CORN (b. 1943)

To a Lover Who is HIV-Positive

You ask what I feel.
Grief; and a hope
that springs from your intention
to forward projects as assertive
or lasting as flesh ever upholds.

Love; and a fear
that the so far implacable
cunning of a virus will smuggle away
substantial warmth, the face, the response
telling us who we are and might be.

Guilt; and bewilderment
that, through no special virtue of mine
or fault of yours, a shadowed affliction
overlooked me and settled on you. As if
all, always, got what was theirs.

Anger; and knowledge
that our venture won't be joined
in perfect safety. Still, it's better odds
than the risk of not feeling much at all.
Until you see yourself well in them,
love, keep looking in my eyes.

ELIZABETH J. COLEMAN (b.1947)

—The One With Violets in Her Lap

after Sappho

is Judy who learned of
her cancer soon
after marriage

At the funeral her step-son
said   so I have this image
of Judy the family is fighting

yelling you know how nasty
these things can be   Judy
goes into the next room sets

the table with a white cloth
edged with lace   puts polished
silver at each place white linen

napkins   a bouquet of calla lilies
tulips roses and daisies
humming to herself then sing-

ing   a small smile on that freckled
face and one by one people wander
from the fighting into Judy's

dining room   Someone lights
the candles –Judy is the one
with violets in her lap

D. H. LAWRENCE (1885–1930)

Brooding Grief

A yellow leaf from the darkness
Hops like a frog before me.
Why should I start and stand still?

I was watching the woman that bore me
Stretched in the brindled darkness
Of the sick-room, rigid with will
To die: and the quick leaf tore me
Back to this rainy swill
Of leaves and lamps and traffic mingled before me.

Voyage

my mother speaks to her sister, Alvina

I never knew your childhood.
You went to live in Cohocton
with Aunt Emily and Uncle Al,
and I was sent to the Hillside Orphanage.
After a decade apart I wondered
if we would ever connect as sisters.

We healed in our twenties,
wore matching dresses to dances at Loon Lake
where suitors paid ten cents each for a chance
to whirl us across the hardwood floor.

We sunned at the beach with wealthy girls
who befriended us. We saved for months
for that cruise to Cuba
on the Swedish boat *Corinthia*.

Wake up, Alvina!
Do you remember the lizards in Havana—
the white uniform you wore to the hospital pharmacy
for almost half a century?

Now, you store trinkets in your old brassieres:
lockets, lace, a keychain from K-Mart.
B-cups make the best containers, you say,
when you can sequence your thoughts.

Last week I found a bra in the bathtub,
a nameless cotton ship
sailing toward the drain
with your dentures in the hold.

Pieces of you
scattered all over the house
a wig in the kitchen, the artificial breast
resting like a flower near the commode.

JENNIFER WALLACE (b. 1954)

Tumor

I set the phone in its cradle and watched a warbler
hopping in the autumn dogwood near the gate.

The bird stopped in my yard on its way to Venezuela.
Miniscule. Dusty yellow. Stripe on its wing.

It could sit in my palm, except the little thing is quick
and I'm ashamed of myself for thinking—

in the midst of admiration for the verve inside its hollow bones—
that I could crush it as I could a piece of paper or a leaf.

But it won't be caught and so I'm saved, though not
for any goodness I possess. When my father said

it was on his liver—10 centimeters by 12, on his liver—
12 seemed too big to be in him, who was big to me

and is big, even now that I am grown. The little warbler
is four inches long. How big is a centimeter?

When I was small he taught me:
to get to inches, we divide by three.

Old Man Travelling

The little hedge-row birds,
That peck along the road, regard him not.
He travels on, and in his face, his step,
His gait, is one expression; every limb,
His look and bending figure, all bespeak
A man who does not move with pain, but moves
With thought—He is insensibly subdued
To settled quiet: he is one by whom
All effort seems forgotten, one to whom
Long patience has such mild composure given,
That patience now doth seem a thing, of which
He hath no need. He is by nature led
To peace so perfect, that the young behold
With envy, what the old man hardly feels.
–I asked him whither he was bound, and what
The object of his journey; he replied
'Sir! I am going many miles to take
A last leave of my son, a mariner,
Who, from a sea-fight has been brought to Falmouth,
And there is dying in an hospital.'

WILLIAM BUTLER YEATS (1865–1939)

A Friend's Illness

Sickness brought me this
Thought, in that scale of his:
Why should I be dismayed
Though flame had burned the whole
World, as it were a coal,
Now I have seen it weighed
Against a soul?

ALICE NOTLEY (b. 1945)

Sonnet

The late Gracie Allen was a very lucid comedienne,
Especially in the way that lucid means shining and bright.
What her husband George Burns called her illogical logic
Made a halo around our syntax and ourselves as we laughed.

George Burns most often was her artful inconspicuous straight man.
He could move people about stage, construct skits and scenes, write
And gather jokes. They were married as long as ordinary magic
Would allow, thirty-eight years, until Gracie Allen's death.

In her fifties Gracie Allen developed a heart condition.
She would call George Burns when her heart felt funny and fluttered
He'd give her a pill and they'd hold each other till the palpitation
Stopped—just a few minutes, many times and pills. As magic fills
Then fulfilled must leave a space, one day Gracie Allen's heart fluttered
And hurt and stopped. George Burns said unbelievingly to the doctor,
    "But I still have some of the pills."

DENISE LEVERTOV (1923–1997)

Talking to Grief

Ah, grief, I should not treat you
like a homeless dog
who comes to the back door
for a crust, for a meatless bone.
I should trust you.

I should coax you
into the house and give you
your own corner,
a worn mat to lie on,
your own water dish.

You think I don't know you've been living
under my porch.
You long for your real place to be readied
before winter comes. You need
your name,
your collar and tag. You need
the right to warn off intruders,
to consider
my house your own
and me your person
and yourself
my own dog

XIII.

HOSPITALS & OTHER PLACES OF HEALING

William Carlos Williams (1883–1963)

Between Walls

the back wings
of the

hospital where
nothing

will grow lie
cinders

in which shine
the broken

pieces of a green
bottle

Jane Mayhall (1918–2009)

Emergency Room Enjoyments

Every relation is a flirtation, an
attraction of cheerful obedience or a
rejection. At New York hospitals, the savage
courtships run rampant, mostly on the indifference side.
When trained nurses have the best opportunity
for practicing the arts of mean treatments,
so clothed in
technological prowess, certificates
of experience and capability, the cold disguise
for punishment and destruction of what
they choose.

In the emergency room, there was
the case of an old shivering woman, brought
with rampant pneumonia, who was left for hours to shiver
and shake with paper towel covering her feet, while the nurses
in their crisp uniforms
exclaimed, she can't have a cover because we don't have
any, and the young physical therapist who brought
the old dame walked miles under the hospital to the basement
laundry where thousands of cozy warm blankets were warming,
and stole one to take back to the emergency room,
of morgue-like extensions,
to keep the dying woman slightly
presentable.

PHILIP LARKIN (1922–1985)

The Building

Higher than the handsomest hotel
The lucent comb shows up for miles, but see,
All round it close-ribbed streets rise and fall
Like a great sigh out of the last century.
The porters are scruffy; what keep drawing up
At the entrance are not taxis; and in the hall
As well as creepers hangs a frightening smell.

There are paperbacks, and tea at so much a cup,
Like an airport lounge, but those who tamely sit
On rows of steel chairs turning the ripped mags
Haven't come far. More like a local bus,
These outdoor clothes and half-filled shopping-bags
And faces restless and resigned, although
Every few minutes comes a kind of nurse

To fetch someone away: the rest refit
Cups back to saucers, cough, or glance below
Seats for dropped gloves or cards. Humans, caught
On ground curiously neutral, homes and names
Suddenly in abeyance; some are young,
Some old, but most at that vague age that claims
The end of choice, the last of hope; and all

Here to confess that something has gone wrong.
It must be error of a serious sort,
For see how many floors it needs, how tall
It's grown by now, and how much money goes
In trying to correct it. See the time,
Half-past eleven on a working day,
And these picked out of it; see, as they climb

To their appointed levels, how their eyes
Go to each other, guessing; on the way
Someone's wheeled past, in washed-to-rags ward clothes:
They see him, too. They're quiet. To realise
This new thing held in common makes them quiet,
For past these doors are rooms, and rooms past those,
And more rooms yet, each one further off

And harder to return from; and who knows
Which he will see, and when? For the moment, wait,
Look down at the yard. Outside seems old enough:
Red brick, lagged pipes, and someone walking by it
Out to the car park, free. Then, past the gate,
Traffic; a locked church; short terraced streets
Where kids chalk games, and girls with hair-dos fetch

Their separates from the cleaners - O world,
Your loves, your chances, are beyond the stretch
Of any hand from here! And so, unreal,
A touching dream to which we all are lulled
But wake from separately. In it, conceits
And self-protecting ignorance congeal
To carry life, collapsing only when

Called to these corridors (for now once more
The nurse beckons—). Each gets up and goes
At last. Some will be out by lunch, or four;
Others, not knowing it, have come to join
The unseen congregations whose white rows
Lie set apart above—women, men;
Old, young; crude facets of the only coin

This place accepts. All know they are going to die.
Not yet, perhaps not here, but in the end,
And somewhere like this. That is what it means,
This clean-sliced cliff; a struggle to transcend
The thought of dying, for unless its powers
Outbuild cathedrals nothing contravenes
The coming dark, though crowds each evening try

With wasteful, weak, propitiatory flowers.

ELIZABETH BISHOP (1911–1979)

Visits to St. Elizabeths

This is the house of Bedlam.

This is the man
that lies in the house of Bedlam.

This is the time
of the tragic man
that lies in the house of Bedlam.

This is a wristwatch
telling the time
of the talkative man
that lies in the house of Bedlam.

This is a sailor
wearing the watch
that tells the time
of the honored man
that lies in the house of Bedlam.

This is the roadstead all of board
reached by the sailor
wearing the watch
that tells the time
of the old, brave man
that lies in the house of Bedlam.

These are the years and the walls of the ward,
the winds and clouds of the sea of board
sailed by the sailor
wearing the watch
that tells the time
of the cranky man
that lies in the house of Bedlam.

This is a Jew in a newspaper hat
that dances weeping down the ward
over the creaking sea of board
beyond the sailor
winding his watch
that tells the time
of the cruel man
that lies in the house of Bedlam.

This is a world of books gone flat.
This is a Jew in a newspaper hat
that dances weeping down the ward
over the creaking sea of board
of the batty sailor
that winds his watch
that tells the time
of the busy man
that lies in the house of Bedlam.

This is a boy that pats the floor
to see if the world is there, is flat,
for the widowed Jew in the newspaper hat
that dances weeping down the ward
waltzing the length of a weaving board
by the silent sailor
that hears his watch
that ticks the time
of the tedious man
that lies in the house of Bedlam.

These are the years and the walls and the door
that shut on a boy that pats the floor
to feel if the world is there and flat.
This is a Jew in a newspaper hat
that dances joyfully down the ward

into the parting seas of board
past the staring sailor
that shakes his watch
that tells the time
of the poet, the man
that lies in the house of Bedlam.

This is the soldier home from the war.
These are the years and the walls and the door
that shut on a boy that pats the floor
to see if the world is round or flat.
This is a Jew in a newspaper hat
that dances carefully down the ward,
walking the plank of a coffin board
with the crazy sailor
that shows his watch
that tells the time
of the wretched man
that lies in the house of Bedlam.

CLARINDA HARRISS (b. 1939)

Union Memorial Hospital

Packed with naked bodies in every posture
of abandon, this must be the most
antisexual place in the world tonight,
this wheezing, dozing hospital
where every half-open door reveals
a waxen homunculus, in a bed
that resembles a torture instrument
or a significant other strewn over
a reclining chair like discarded clothes.
Awful holes emitting snores or apparatus.
Worst, the parodies of veins suspended
in clear plastic tubing from above
while parodies of bowels gnarl around bedlegs.

A persistent friction, the tug of a tube
scotchtaped to my crotch

must, therefore, explain why
in this Temple of Anaphrodisia I
find I'm counting myself to sleep
with old lovers' names, counting how many
love positions the mechanical
bed could twist a body into
by the right touch

of the Head Foot Up Down buttons,
finally counting the fluorescent stars
in the sexy downtown skyline—
having thrown the drapes back from
the wall-size window in my room
to give the whole city a wink at
my backless nightgown.

L. E. Sissman (1928–1976)

A Deathplace

Very few people know where they will die,
But I do: in a brick-faced hospital,
Divided, not unlike Caesarean Gaul,
Into three parts: the Dean Memorial
Wing, in the classic cast of 1910,
Green-grated in unglazed, Aeolian
Embrasures; the Maud Wiggin Building, which
Commemorates a dog-jawed Boston bitch
Who fought the brass down to their whipcord knees
In World War I, and won enlisted men
Some decent hospitals, and, being rich,
Donated her own granite monument;
The Mandeville Pavilion, pink-brick tent
With marble piping, flying snapping flags
Above the entry where our bloody rags
Are rolled in to be sponged and sewn again.
Today is fair; tomorrow, scourging rain
(If only my own tears) will see me in
Those jaundiced and distempered corridors
Off which the five-foot-wide doors slowly close.
White as my skimpy chiton, I will cringe
Before the pinpoint of the least syringe;
Before the buttered catheter goes in;
Before the I.V.'s lisp and drip begins
Inside my skin; before the rubber hand
Upon the lancet takes aim and descends
To lay me open, and upon its thumb
Retracts the trouble, a malignant plum;
And finally, I'll quail before the hour
When the authorities shut off the power
In that vast hospital, and in my bed
I'll feel my blood go thin, go white, the red,
The rose all leached away, and I'll go dead.
Then will the business of life resume:
The muffled trolley wheeled into my room,

The off-white blanket blanking off my face,
The stealing secret, private, *largo* race
Down halls and elevators to the place
I'll be consigned to for transshipment, cased
In artificial air and light: the ward
That's underground; the terminal; the morgue.
Then one fine day when all the smart flags flap,
A booted man in black with a peaked cap
Will call for me and troll me down the hall
And slot me into his black car. That's all.

GREY GOWRIE (b. 1939)

The Third Day

Respirators sound like trout feeding
at night in some dream hatchery—no one there
to listen; our subaqueous world of care
is halfway blue—peaceful, unthreatening.

Spectacles pressed to the glass, our specialists
walk by to look us over and seem the same
until, mask-mouthed, they enter: clipboard lists
distinguish the paraphernalia from the name.

We are our medication, and the machines
programmed to meet an individual case
more than identity now. We may have been;
some may become again. We have no face

to lose, to look at, but it's pleasant here,
suspense suspended, nothing to be done
for the time being—time being our time won
to flail for birth again and fight for air.

WILLIAM MATTHEWS (1942–1997)

Orthopedic Surgery Ward

And what else? The rain-headed cars in rows,
the pale, foreshortened city awash on the gray
horizon, two skeletal poplars, an unslaked sky.

On the bed next to mine, an old man dying,
adrift on a thermal of morphine. And I, less ill
by far but rancid with boredom, holding my bad

leg numb and still. The day seems like a long
choral breath—some of us are casual, some wheeze
and strain, a few are dictated to by machines.

Now the rain, and now the light comes at a slant
from the west. At night the hale lie down, too,
though a few are chosen to watch for us all,

to monitor the machines that monitor the sick
while loneliness, complacent and businesslike,
conducts its brisk, meticulous rounds.

Robert Lowell (1917–1977)

Waking in the Blue

The night attendant, a B.U. sophomore,
rouses from the mare's-nest of his drowsy head
propped on *The Meaning of Meaning*.
He catwalks down our corridor.
Azure day
makes my agonized blue window bleaker.
Crows maunder on the petrified fairway.
Absence! My hearts grows tense
as though a harpoon were sparring for the kill.
(This is the house for the "mentally ill.")

What use is my sense of humor?
I grin at Stanley, now sunk in his sixties,
once a Harvard all-American fullback,
(if such were possible!)
still hoarding the build of a boy in his twenties,
as he soaks, a ramrod
with a muscle of a seal
in his long tub,
vaguely urinous from the Victorian plumbing.
A kingly granite profile in a crimson golf-cap,
worn all day, all night,
he thinks only of his figure,
of slimming on sherbert and ginger ale—
more cut off from words than a seal.

This is the way day breaks in Bowditch Hall at McLean's;
the hooded night lights bring out "Bobbie,"
Porcellian '29,
a replica of Louis XVI
without the wig—
redolent and roly-poly as a sperm whale,
as he swashbuckles about in his birthday suit
and horses at chairs.

These victorious figures of bravado ossified young.

In between the limits of day,
hours and hours go by under the crew haircuts
and slightly too little nonsensical bachelor twinkle
of the Roman Catholic attendants.
(There are no Mayflower
screwballs in the Catholic Church.)

After a hearty New England breakfast,
I weigh two hundred pounds
this morning. Cock of the walk,
I strut in my turtle-necked French sailor's jersey
before the metal shaving mirrors,
and see the shaky future grow familiar
in the pinched, indigenous faces
of these thoroughbred mental cases,
twice my age and half my weight.
We are all old-timers,
each of us holds a locked razor.

KELLY CHERRY (b. 1940)

In the Place Where the Corridors Watch
Your Every Move

In the place where the corridors watch your every move,
In the place of the gossiping psychiatrists who pass
What their patients say around like children playing
Telephone, until the message that said *Help me* has become
The sky has disappeared, leaving nothing in its place,

In the place where bewigged judges disguise themselves as bearded
    psychiatrists,
In the place of rooms that do not lock and of rooms that lock
Only from the outside, in the place of misery beyond telling, in the
    place of weeping
And white fluted flowers that bloom in trays at regular hours, a pink or
    blue
Or golden seed splitting at its heart while the corridors watch your
    every move,

In the place of the talking doctors whose definitions are all synonyms
And the place of the patients who have nothing to say, since what the
    patients say,
The doctors translate, thinking, because they have been given degrees
    and because
Their dictionaries may be modified by majority vote at the APA, that
    they understand
The language, in the place where the corridors watch your every move,

Someone was saying *Help me help me I am frightened*
Because the sky has disappeared, leaving nothing in its place.

TOM SLEIGH (b. 1953)

Clinic

The name the nurse calls ripples down the corridor:
unspoken privacies speak in the women's eyes
as their anxious hands, lifting to their hair, freeze

as if caught in the convex mirror by an unseen painter
who, if he chooses, can paint into being cheeks of fat,
heart, lungs, spinal cord that sparks the birth-cry

still wawling in the younger women's futures;
while for others the lucent ovum won't darken
again with sperm . . . Queenly bulk still hidden,

these bellies won't stretch into globes
whose latitudes will be lavish
as the ermine-trimmed velvet robe

of the young, pale bride, her husband's face gravely
tender, his hand on her hand on her bulging belly
shadowed by death from septicemia.

In the young women's ears "the procedure" whispers
protocols—and in one older one's, her cheekbones
round and high as the painted girl-wife who will die;

the younger ones look up at her, her crowsfeet
attractive in a face so kind
that the others' sidelong stares look startled . . .

Outside, no picketers carry signs
neatly scrawled in red crayon by their own children:
SUFFER THE LITTLE CHILDREN TO COME UNTO ME!!!

Dust spirals into a double helix interlacing
across sunglare in the waiting room mirror
as the blinds rule out the cool March light in a gridiron

that crosses the older one's face and hands:
the clinic door beckons, the nurse again calls her name,
she wades through the television's low-voiced drone.

The room pitching and rolling in waves of neon
is like a ship on the horizon sailing into the sun
as into the too bright dream of the merchant husband,

his child-wife's face and his baby's face come streaming
across the reef ripping the hull, splintering, grinding—
all this is written in the papers of the young merchant

grown old along with his second wife
and their two daughters married in 1456 and 1459
"to sons with no insufficient dowries"...

And now, it's your turn—you walk through the clinic door,
your beauty's not untouchable, you are a woman in a woman's body
in your jeans and gray sweatshirt and pink sneakers,

you move down the hall to the examining room, you put
on your gown, the anaesthetic numbs but not enough
not to feel the vacuum hurt as walls fall away and you're out

walking among vegetable stalls, the blinding canals floating
red madder dyes, a persimmon brought back from countries
of the sun, a leek, a lopped turnip top flashing bright green.

EDWARD HIRSCH (b. 1950)

Skywriting

(Harper Grace Hospital, July 15, 1984)

Through the west window
                    I could see a fractured moon
Installed in the smokestacks behind the house,
Almost full, frail in the half-rain, half-mist
Of a midsummer twilight
                    that lingered for a long time
On the slanted roofs
                and died on the black top of the river.

All afternoon my friend slept—
                his breathing labored, dogged, intense—
As the colors visibly
              out of the air-conditioned air
(A steady sifting of purples and blues,
                  bloodless oranges and pinks)
While darkness thickened on the white walls
And shadows crept like a judgment on the floor.

It's hard to bring back
              the slow terror of that afternoon
In a sterile place, my friend's dream
Of health drifting further and further away
From his body,
           almost palpable in the cool air,
A cloud above his head,
           the breath stuttering in his lungs. . . .

For me, it was like being called to the window
To see our two bodies in the rainy light
             of a darkness falling,
The faint, bluish-white twins
        of Gemini rising

And splitting apart,

                    a barge pulling a single star

Over the swollen, accidental faces of trees.

That night I saw living and dying in everything,

Even in the long bands of light

                            climbing out of the water,

One rainbow penetrating the night sky

While a second one arched

                  over its spectral head,

The bodies luminous and doubled,

                      their colors reversed.

SHIRLEY J. BREWER (b. 1947)

Lament

I UNION MEMORIAL HOSPITAL
   Baltimore, Maryland
   March, 1993   Room 6640

You stayed with me for eight weeks
after my surgery. Eighty and spry,
you lamented your lack of a driver's license,
although my friends vied
for a chance to chauffeur you.
In the hospital, you fussed
over my IV tubes, brought me muffins.
They sent me home before the big snow;
we hibernated, read the same mysteries.
Mother and daughter—you cooked, I healed.
Looking back, I thought I'd remember pain,
my long scar. Instead, I saw you
in my hospital room, your smile, the way
you fluffed my pillows.

II UNITY HOSPITAL
   Rochester, New York
   January, 2009   Room 2209

I stayed with you those last four days,
while snow piled up like polar bear rugs
around the hospital. You refused
the glazed doughnuts you loved,
retreated behind an oxygen mask,
each breath a solemn sound.
I read you poems, kept talking,
afraid of too much silence.
I wanted to drive a getaway car,
whisk you off to Atlantic City and Cape May.

Instead, I held your hand, touched
your delicate skin.
Outside your window, snow kept falling—
nothing I could do to stop it.

HOWARD NEMEROV (1920–1991)

Near the Old People's Home

The people on the avenue at noon,
Sharing the sparrows and the wintry sun,
The turned-off fountain with its basin drained
And cement benches etched with checkerboards,

Are old and poor, most every one of them
Wearing some decoration of his damage,
Bandage or crutch or cane; and some are blind,
Or nearly, tap-tapping along with white wands.

When they open their mouths, there are no teeth.
All the same, they keep on talking to themselves
Even while bending to hawk up spit or blood
In gutters that will be there when they are gone.

Some have the habit of getting hit by cars
Three times a year; the ambulance comes up
And away they go, mumbling even in shock
The many secret names they have for God.

LOUISE BOGAN (1897–1970)

Evening in the Sanitarium

The free evening fades, outside the windows fastened with decorative
    iron grilles.
The lamps are lighted; the shades drawn; the nurses are watching a little.
It is the hour of the complicated knitting on the safe bone needles; of
    the games of anagrams and bridge;
The deadly game of chess; the book held up like a mask.

The period of the wildest weeping, the fiercest delusion, is over.
The women rest their tired half-healed hearts; they are almost well.
Some of them will stay almost well always: the blunt-faced woman
    whose thinking dissolved
Under academic discipline; the manic-depressive girl
Now leveling off; one paranoiac afflicted with jealousy.
Another with persecution. Some alleviation has been possible.

O fortunate bride, who never again will become elated after childbirth!
O lucky older wife, who has been cured of feeling unwanted!
To the suburban railway station you will return, return,
To meet forever Jim home on the 5:35.
You will be again as normal and selfish and heartless as anybody else.

There is life left: the piano says it with its octave smile.
The soft carpets pad the thump and splinter of the suicide to be.
Everything will be splendid: the grandmother will not drink habitually.
The fruit salad will bloom on the plate like a bouquet
And the garden produce the blue-ribbon aquilegia.
The cats will be glad; the fathers feel justified; the mothers relieved.
The sons and husbands will no longer need to pay the bills.
Childhoods will be put away, the obscene nightmare abated.

At the ends of the corridors the baths are running.
Mrs. C. again feels the shadow of the obsessive idea.
Miss R. looks at the mantel-piece, which must mean something.

ANYA SILVER (b. 1968)

Leaving the Hospital

As the doors glide shut behind me,
the world flares back into being—
I exist again, recover myself,
sunlight undimmed by dark panes,
the heat on my arms the earth's breath.
The wind tongues me to my feet
like a doe licking her newborn fawn.
At my back, days measured by vital signs,
my mouth opened and arm extended,
the nighttime cries of a man withered
child-size by cancer, and the bells
of emptied IVs tolling through hallways.
Before me, life—mysterious, ordinary—
holding off pain with its muscular wings.
Stepping to the curb, an orange moth
dives into the basket of roses
that lately stood on my sick room table,
and the petals yield to its persistent
nudge, opening manifold and golden

XIV.

Convalescence

RUTH STONE (1915–2011)

Healing

for Pheobe

Last night the children were here.
I went to bed before they left.
When I got up this morning
The house was brilliant;
Every light flashed its own sun;
Not a bulb burned out
But all sent ohms striking
The dust with the gaiety of headlong
Burning. And in the kitchen
The glorious remains of snacks
And little meals spread the color
Of tomatoes, onion peels;
The savory abandon
Of bodies heated.
All their energy lay about me
As I went in my pale gown
From lamp to lamp
Pulling the cords
And thinking
What delicious sleep I had;
I am not even sick any more.

WILLIAM CARLOS WILLIAMS (1883–1963)

The World Contracted to a Recognizable Image

at the small end of an illness
there was a picture
probably Japanese
which filled my eye

an idiotic picture
except it was all I recognized
the wall lived for me in that picture
I clung to it as a fly

D. H. LAWRENCE (1885–1930)

Healing

I am not a mechanism, an assembly of various sections.
And it is not because the mechanism is working wrongly, that I am ill.
I am ill because of wounds to the soul, to the deep emotional self
and the wounds to the soul take a long, long time, only time can help
and patience, and a certain difficult repentance
long, difficult repentance, realization of life's mistake, and the freeing
    oneself
from the endless repetition of the mistake
which mankind at large has chosen to sanctify.

Thomas Hardy (1840–1928)

A Wasted Illness

Through vaults of pain,
Enribbed and wrought with groins of ghastliness,
I passed, and garish spectres moved my brain
            To dire distress.

And hammerings,
            And quakes, and shoots, and stifling hotness, blent
With webby waxing things and waning things
            As on I went.

"Where lies the end
To this foul way?" I asked with weakening breath.
Thereon ahead I saw a door extend—
            The door to Death.

It loomed more clear:
"At last!" I cried. "The all-delivering door!"
And then, I knew not how, it grew less near
            Than theretofore.

And back slid I
Along the galleries by which I came,
And tediously the day returned, and sky,
            And life—the same.

And all was well:
Old circumstance resumed its former show,
And on my head the dews of comfort fell
            As ere my woe.

I roam anew,
Scarce conscious of my late distress.... And yet
Those backward steps to strength I cannot view
            Without regret.

For that dire train
Of waxing shapes and waning, passed before,
And those grim aisles, must be ranged again
To reach that door

Sylvia Plath (1932–1963)

In Plaster

I shall never get out of this! There are two of me now:
This new absolutely white person and the old yellow one,
And the white person is certainly the superior one.
She doesn't need food, she is one of the real saints.
At the beginning I hated her, she had no personality—
She lay in bed with me like a dead body
And I was scared, because she was shaped just the way I was

Only much whiter and unbreakable and with no complaints.
I couldn't sleep for a week, she was so cold.
I blamed her for everything, but she didn't answer.
I couldn't understand her stupid behavior!
When I hit her she held still, like a true pacifist.
Then I realized what she wanted was for me to love her:
She began to warm up, and I saw her advantages.

Without me, she wouldn't exist, so of course she was grateful.
I gave her a soul, I bloomed out of her as a rose
Blooms out of a vase of not very valuable porcelain,
And it was I who attracted everybody's attention,
Not her whiteness and beauty, as I had at first supposed.
I patronized her a little, and she lapped it up—
You could tell almost at once she had a slave mentality.

I didn't mind her waiting on me, and she adored it.
In the morning she woke me early, reflecting the sun
From her amazingly white torso, and I couldn't help but notice
Her tidiness and her calmness and her patience:
She humored my weakness like the best of nurses,
Holding my bones in place so they would mend properly.
In time our relationship grew more intense.

She stopped fitting me so closely and seemed offish.
I felt her criticizing me in spite of herself,
As if my habits offended her in some way.
She let in the drafts and became more and more absent-minded.
And my skin itched and flaked away in soft pieces
Simply because she looked after me so badly.
Then I saw what the trouble was: she thought she was immortal.

She wanted to leave me, she thought she was superior,
And I'd been keeping her in the dark, and she was resentful—
Wasting her days waiting on a half-corpse!
And secretly she began to hope I'd die.
Then she could cover my mouth and eyes, cover me entirely,
And wear my painted face the way a mummy-case
Wears the face of a pharaoh, though it's made of mud and water.

I wasn't in any position to get rid of her.
She'd supported me for so long I was quite limp—
I had forgotten how to walk or sit,
So I was careful not to upset her in any way
Or brag ahead of time how I'd avenge myself.
Living with her was like living with my own coffin:
Yet I still depended on her, though I did it regretfully.

I used to think we might make a go of it together—
After all, it was a kind of marriage, being so close.
Now I see it must be one or the other of us.
She may be a saint, and I may be ugly and hairy,
But she'll soon find out that that doesn't matter a bit.
I'm collecting my strength; one day I shall manage without her,
And she'll perish with emptiness then, and begin to miss me.

SHIRLEY J. BREWER (b. 1947)

Setback

A goddess in gold earrings and a walker,
my feet stutter along hospital floors,

while my mind conjures rhinestone
stilettos, my pelvis whole again.

I'll trade these non-skid socks
for silk stockings that shimmer in the dark.

When my bones heal,
I'll shop for sandals with sequins,

slingbacks. I'll sway and strut in six-inch heels,
pivot like a model dazzling the runway.

Oh, tango shoes with red satin straps,
lift me up, release me.

DAVID BERGMAN (b. 1950)

The Beauty of Convalescence

Even more than in childhood, I have learned to appreciate
the beauty of convalescence.
                  —Victor Brombert

The beauty of convalescence is known
Only to those who have been gravely ill
And have lost the drive to be well again.

It is they who can let wakefulness brew
In the heat of sleep until it grows tawny
With light and cool enough to drink.

They can hear voices in another room
And footsteps in the hallway and be content
With no word understood, the door unopened.

The body drifts in its own currents, feeling
Here a root of an old tree, there the boot
Of an angler dropping his scrawny worm

Into the waiting mouths of the walleyed
And insatiable. The books one reads are
Remembered for the way the pages were filled

With print, the stiffness of the binding, and how
The words colluded with dreams to simulate
A life all the more distant because things

happened there and had consequence. The beauty
Of convalescence is the discovery that stillness
Is a form in need of recovery

In which time repairs itself. Those who appreciate
Its pleasure must give up waiting to be healed.
They must learn that it's best to slip back into

The soothing void where you can do nothing
More than remain where you are, and even that
Should be too much for anyone to ask of you.

The first few steps around the room, the hour
Sitting in the garden watching the dogs
Romp through the tender grass after the ball

You've not the strength to throw, these are the last
Moments you have to convalesce. Your doctors,
Friends and so-called loved ones have been planning

All along your return to your former life.
Soon they'll order exercise and treatment;
They will place you on a regimen back

To your old restlessness and dissatisfaction.
You'll be pressured into being well, taught
To forget about dying. They'll make you

Believe once more in your immortality.
Don't bother to resist. Ignoring them
Is itself a sign of renewed energy.

You have no choice but relinquish your treasured
Convalescence you had no right to and face
With grace the ugliness that passes for health.

MARK DOTY (b. 1953)

The Embrace

You weren't well or really ill yet either;
just a little tired, your handsomeness
tinged by grief or anticipation, which brought
to your face a thoughtful, deepening grace.

I didn't for a moment doubt you were dead.
I knew that to be true still, even in the dream.
You'd been out—at work maybe?—
having a good day, almost energetic.

We seemed to be moving from some old house
where we'd lived, boxes everywhere, things
in disarray: that was the *story* of my dream,
but even asleep I was shocked out of narrative

by your face, the physical fact of your face:
inches from mine, smooth-shaven, loving, alert.
Why so difficult, remembering the actual look
of you? Without a photograph, without strain?

So when I saw your unguarded, reliable face,
your unmistakable gaze opening all the warmth
and clarity of you—warm brown tea—we held
each other for the time the dream allowed.

Bless you. You came back, so I could see you
once more, plainly, so I could rest against you
without thinking this happiness lessened anything,
without thinking you were alive again.

ELIZABETH J. COLEMAN (b. 1947)

And I Want to Start Again

I ride backward on the train: face
the guy replacing me
talk about problems that are no longer mine.

And I'm a zebra running in the season
of great migration in the Bush. I'm the turkey
spared by the President on Thanksgiving.
I'm the pigeon that didn't get run over by the SUV;
the rat that found the square of bread left
by a homeless man in the subway.

It took moxie to walk away, a colleague says.
How I love that word, born
of a soft drink.
But it wasn't so much moxie talking
as a brush with cancer.

I'd like grandchildren or at least a dog,
try to remember that Buddhist idea that all
the dogs on the street are mine and
everybody's, and things don't belong to us.

Then I picture the photo of my children
sitting on the grass with the Eiffel Tower
in the background when we were young
and making dumb mistakes, and I want to start again.

ROBERT LOWELL (1917–1977)

Home After Three Months Away

Gone now the baby's nurse,
a lioness who ruled the roost
and made the Mother cry.
She used to tie
gobbets of porkrind in bowknots of gauze—
three months they hung like soggy toast
on our eight foot magnolia tree,
and helped the English sparrows
weather a Boston winter.

Three months, three months!
Is Richard now himself again?
Dimpled with exaltation,
my daughter holds her levee in the tub.
Our noses rub,
each of us pats a stringy lock of hair—
they tell me nothing's gone.
Though I am forty-one,
not forty now, the time I put away
was child's play. After thirteen weeks
my child still dabs her cheeks
to start me shaving. When
we dress her in her sky-blue corduroy,
she changes to a boy,
and floats my shaving brush
and washcloth in the flush. . . .
Dearest I cannot loiter here
in lather like a polar bear.

Recuperating, I neither spin nor toil.
Three stories down below,
a choreman tends our coffin's length of soil,
and seven horizontal tulips blow.
Just twelve months ago,
these flowers were pedigreed

imported Dutchmen; now no one need
distinguish them from weed.
Bushed by the late spring snow,
they cannot meet
another year's snowballing enervation.

I keep no rank nor station.
Cured, I am frizzled, stale and small.

MARY JO SALTER (b. 1954)

Half a Double Sonnet

for Ben

Their ordeal over, now the only trouble
was conveying somehow to a boy of three
that for a week or two he'd be seeing double.
Surely he wouldn't recall the surgery
years later, but what about the psychic scars?
And so, when the patch came off, they bought the toy
he'd wanted most. He held it high. "Two cars!"
he cried; and drove himself from joy to joy.
Two baby sisters . . . One was enough of Clare,
but who could complain?—considering that another
woman had stepped forward to take care
of the girls, which left him all alone with Mother.
Victory! Even when he went to pee,
he was seconded in his virility.

FLOYD SKLOOT (b. 1947)

Channel

In time the fork my life took
as illness changed its course
will wander to the main stream
and there below the long waterfalls
and cataracts I will begin my rush
to the place I was going from the start.
I imagine looking back to see
the silted mass where a huge bend
holds sunlight in a net of evergreen
and the sky unable to bear its own
violet brilliance a moment longer.
Out of shadows where the channel
crumbles comes the raucous sound
a great blue heron makes when startled.
Scent of peppermint rides breezes
from the valley and I catch hints
of current beneath the surface
just as darkness unfurls.
There I imagine what was lost
coming together with what was gained
to pour itself at last into the sea.

EDWARD HIRSCH (b. 1950)

Recovery

It was as if the rain could feel itself
falling through the air today, as if the air
could actually feel its own dampness, the breeze
could hear a familiar voice explaining the emptiness
to the dark elms that swayed unconsciously along
the wet road, the elms that could still feel
their own branches glistening with rain.

It was as if the sky had imagined a morning
of indigos and pinks, mauves and reddish-browns.
The smiling young nurse who helped you into the car
was wearing two colorful ribbons in her auburn hair and
somehow they looked precisely like ribbons gleaming
in the hair of a woman helping you into a car.
I believe I had never seen ribbons before.

And suddenly I was staring at asphalt
puddle with rainwater. And bluish letters
purpling on a white sign. And sliding electric
ENTRANCES & EXITS. And statues bristling with color.
The yellow sunlight filtered through the clouds
and I believe I had never seen a street lamp
shimmer across a wavy puddle before.

The road home was slick with lights
and everything seemed to be crying, *just
this, just this, nothing more, nothing else!*—
as if the morning were somehow conscious of itself.
When you leaned over and touched me on the arm
it was as if my arm needed to be touched
in that way, at exactly that time.

GRACE SCHULMAN (b. 1935)

Walk!

Arise, and take up thy bed, and walk.
—Mark 2:9

Rise up and stagger now on the sea road
at sunset, where clouds vanish like bandages

that fall from cured flesh, where lavender nods.
Wade through wild roses poking up through sand.

At low tide, a green island looms so close
that, though fumbling, you might trudge through water,

never mind leap or glide, and reach dry sand.
Once you strode high, unbending, and you fell

like a tree. When strangers helped you rise,
a smile masked rage. Science your guide, you'd been

the healer, not the healed. Days of rain
when others shot the stairs, leaped into waves,

swam inlets. Bend to the knife. And even after,
you said, no miracle. A surgeon's skill.

But here are wonders. You limp past scrub pines
and hear the salt wind play a lyre-shaped oak.

Wake to flaws; the sea tosses back shells
brightest when they are chipped, snapped, and broken.

Queen Hermione, perfect in stone,
stirs, steps off a fluted post, and stumbles,

never to soar. We slog. We tramp the road
of possibility. Give me your arm.

ENVOI

A book of this size and scope would not be possible without the help and collaboration of many special people. The early and enthusiastic support of poet-friends such as Ed Hirsch, mentors Tom Lux and Dick Allen, Stanley Plumly, Grace Schulman, and past poet laureates William Jay Smith and the late Daniel Hoffman, was critical in the recruitment of other distinguished contributors to the project. I am grateful for what I learned during many fruitful summers spent at the Writing Seminars at Sarah Lawrence College and the subsequent participation of Vijay Seshadri and Dennis Nurkse. Special thanks to Tree Swenson, former director of the American Academy of Poets, for sensitive editing and early publication of a shortened version of the Introductory essay for this book on the web site of the Academy.

At Persea, the support of publisher Michael Braziller was critical to the efforts of a neophyte anthologist such as myself. So too the hard work of editor Gabriel Fried and his industrious band of student interns at the University of Missouri. The permissions process for such a book is highly complex; in this regard, I was fortunate to have the services of Fred Courtright, a man who seems to know everything about permissions. I would be remiss in not mentioning an experienced anthologist and dear friend, Helen Houghton, who introduced me to Persea Books, to Tree Swenson and to Fred.

Throughout the many years involved I had the unstinting advice and support, emotional and otherwise, of my wife and close collaborator Ilene Salcman. Only she shared the vicissitudes of the effort involved. Only I can know how many errors were prevented or corrected by the advice of friends and colleagues. The responsibility for any remaining imperfections is entirely mine; the book could have easily been twice as large and still considered incomplete. As both physician and poet I am well aware of how often perfection is the enemy of the good; as teachers and as human beings, we are students all our lives. This book represents the realization of a long-standing dream and is dedicated to my most important teachers, my patients and my students in the arts and sciences.

—MS

NOTES ON THE POETS

DANNIE ABSE (b.1923) is a pulmonologist and writer, the author of novels, plays, and nearly twenty books of poetry. He was made a Fellow of the Royal Society of Literature in 1983 and named a Commander of the British Empire in 2013.

DICK ALLEN (b.1939) is currently poet laureate of Connecticut. His awards include the Robert Frost Prize for Poetry, the Hart Crane Poetry Prize, and the May Caroline Davis Poetry Prize from the Poetry Society of America.

YEHUDA AMICHAI (1924–2000) is widely considered to be Israel's most important modern poet. Born in Wurzburg, Germany, he immigrated to Palestine in 1936. In 1982, he received the Israel Prize for Poetry; in 1986 he became an honorary member of the American Academy of Arts and Letters.

PHILIP APPLEMAN (b.1926) has spent much of his later career writing about Charles Darwin. He is the author of three novels, five books of poetry, and six volumes of nonfiction.

ELIZABETH ARNOLD (b.1958) has published two books of poems and teaches in the MFA program at the University of Maryland.

W. H. AUDEN (1907–1973) was born in York, England, the son of a physician. He moved to the United States in 1939 and became an American citizen. The author of numerous books and libretti, he is among the greatest English-language poets of the twentieth century.

CHARLES BAUDELAIRE (1821–1867) is the inventor of the prose poem and the father of Symbolist poetry. He also created the first body of great urban poetry and the concept of the *flâneur*, the walker who observes urban life. His most famous poetic work is *Les Fleurs du Mal* (*The Flowers of Evil*).

THOMAS LOVELL BEDDOES (1803–1849) was an English poet who studied medicine in Germany. He was obsessed with graves, death and the supernatural. He struggled with manic depression and alcoholism, and died by suicide.

COLEMAN BARKS (b.1937) is a poet and acclaimed translator of the Persian poet Rumi. He taught for thirty years at the University of Georgia.

GOTTFRIED BENN (1886–1956) was the most important physician-poet in the German language. He worked as a dermatologist and treated venereal diseases in Berlin.

DAVID BERGMAN (b.1950) teaches at Towson University in Baltimore. His *Cracking The Code* won the George Elliston Prize.

JOHN BERRYMAN (1914–1972) was an essential Confessional poet. His 77 *Dream Songs* won the Pulitzer Prize. Berryman's father committed suicide, and the poet battled depression and alcohol all his life; he jumped off a bridge at the University of Minnesota and died in a frozen pond.

ELIZABETH BISHOP (1911–1979) is one of the most revered American poets of the twentieth century. She received numerous recognitions for her work, including a National Book Award and a Pulitzer Prize. She was Poetry Consultant to the Library of Congress from 1949–50. Bishop once said that her dream had been to write pop songs and go to medical school; her father died from Bright's Disease and her mother went mad.

WILLIAM BLAKE (1757–1827) was the only one of history's greatest painters to also be one of its greatest poets. He invented a type of engraving that allowed him to combine his poems and drawings on a single sheet.

LOUISE BOGAN (1897–1970) was a poet and the longtime poetry editor of *The New Yorker*. She served as Poetry Consultant to the Library of Congress in 1945–46.

EAVAN BOLAND (b. 1944), a native of Dublin, teaches at Stanford University, where she directs the Wallace Stegner Fellowship Program. She is the author of numerous collections of poetry, most recently *A Woman Without a Country*, as well as a number of books of nonfiction.

SHIRLEY J. BREWER (b. 1947) worked for thirty years as a speech therapist. She is the author of a poetry collection, *A Little Breast Music*.

JOHN BRICUTH (JOHN IRWIN, b. 1940) is the Decker Professor in the Humanities and Professor in The Writing Seminars and the English Department of The Johns Hopkins University. He is the author of many critical and poetical works, including *As Long As It's Big: A Narrative Poem*.

RAFAEL CAMPO (b. 1964) is a physician at Harvard Medical School and the Beth Israel Deaconess Medical Center in Boston. He is a recipient of the National Hispanic Academy of Arts and Sciences Annual Achievement Award and two Lambda Literary Awards. In addition to five collections of poetry, he is the author of two prose books: *The Healing Art: A Doctor's Black Bag of Poetry* and *The Poetry of Healing*, a memoir.

C. P. CAVAFY (1863–1933) spent most of his life in Alexandria, Egypt, the city of his birth but, like Cleopatra, was of Greek origin; he is generally considered the finest Greek poet of the modern era. Cavafy lived above a bordello from where he could see a church and the central hospital of his city.

GEOFFREY CHAUCER (1343–1400) was the first great poet of the English language. He served Edward III, who granted him a gallon of wine a day for life, in effect making him the first poet laureate. He began work on *The Canterbury Tales* in the 1380s, and shared the Italian poet Petrarch's skeptical attitude towards medicine.

KELLY CHERRY (b. 1940), named poet laureate of Virginia in 2010, is the author of many books. She is the first winner of the Hanes Poetry Prize, and taught at the University of Wisconsin-Madison for many years.

AMY CLAMPITT (1920–1994) did not publish her first full-length collection until she was 63. Clampitt lived in New York, where she worked for Oxford University Press.

LUCILLE CLIFTON (1936–2010), a former poet laureate of Maryland, won the National Book Award for *Blessing the Boats*. Among her varied poetic subjects were her battles with diabetes, cancer and kidney disease.

ELIZABETH J. COLEMAN (b. 1947) has published poems in the *Connecticut Review*, *Per Contra*, *32 Poems* and other journals.

ROBERT COOPERMAN (b. 1946) is the author of more than 10 volumes of poetry, including *Petitions for Immortality: Scenes from the Life of John Keats*.

ALFRED CORN (b. 1943) is a poet, essayist, novelist, and art critic. He is the author of numerous books of poetry, as well as *The Poem's Heartbeat*, a manual on prosody. His later poems have been deeply influenced by AIDS-related illnesses in his friends.

SARAH N. CROSS (b. 1977) won the William Carlos Williams Poetry Competition as a medical student at the University Chicago. She practices obstetrics-gynecology at Yale.

E. E. CUMMINGS (1894–1962) was an innovative and decorated American poet, recipient of numerous recognitions, including an Academy of American Poets Fellowship, two Guggenheim Fellowships, the Charles Eliot Norton Professorship at Harvard, the Bollingen Prize in Poetry, and a Ford Foundation grant.

CORTNEY DAVIS (b. 1945), a nurse practitioner, is the author of five poetry collections, most recently *Leopold's Maneuvers*, winner of the *Prairie Schooner* Book Award. Her non-fiction publications include *The Heart's Truth: Essays on the Art of Nursing*, winner of the *American Journal of Nursing* Book of the Year Award, and *When the Nurse Becomes a Patient: a Story in Words and Images*. She is poetry editor of the journal *Alimentum: the Literature of Food*.

EMILY DICKINSON (1830–1886) is widely considered to be, with Walt Whitman, America's greatest poet. Many of her poems deal with illness, death, and the body.

SHARON DOLIN (b. 1956) is the author of five books of poetry, and the recipient of a 2013 Witter Bynner Fellowship from the Library of Congress. She directs the Center for Book Arts Annual Letterpress Poetry Chapbook Competition.

JOHN DONNE (1572–1631), the leading Metaphysical poet, was born in London. He was unable to obtain a degree from Oxford or Cambridge because of his Catholicism. Donne became a lawyer and priest, and lived in poverty all his life. His early satires employ images of sickness, vomit, and plague.

MARK DOTY (b. 1953) is one of America's most distinguished poets. *Fire to Fire:*

New and Selected Poems won the National Book Award. He has also won the T. S. Eliot Prize and a National Book Critics Circle Award. He teaches at Rutgers University in New Jersey.

SIR ARTHUR CONAN DOYLE (1859–1930), an assistant chronicler for the adventures of the world's first consulting detective, studied medicine at Edinburgh and became an unsuccessful Harley Street ophthalmologist. His descriptions of Dr. Watson's immortal detective friend are based on Doyle's professor of pathology, Dr. Bell. After his son died, he gave up science and literature for spiritualism.

STEPHEN DUNN (b. 1939) lives and works in Frostburg, Maryland. He won the Pulitzer Prize for *Different Hours*.

T. S. ELIOT (1888–1965), the essential Modernist poet, was born in St. Louis, educated at Harvard and immigrated to England. In 1949, he won the Nobel Prize in Literature. He died of emphysema.

CLAUDIA EMERSON (1957–2014) was the author of a number of poetry collections, including *Late Wife* (2006), which won the Pulitzer Prize. She was named Virginia's poet laureate in 2008.

WILLIAM EMPSON (1906–1984) was born in Yorkshire. An important critic as well as a poet, his practice of close reading was fundamental to the New Criticism.

DANIEL MARK EPSTEIN (b. 1948) is a poet, playwright, and biographer. He has received a Guggenheim Fellowship and is a recent winner of an Academy Award in Literature from the Academy of Arts and Sciences.

B. H. FAIRCHILD (b. 1942) is the author of five collections of poetry, including *The Art of The Lathe*, which won the Kingsley Tufts Award, and *The Blue Buick: New and Selected Poems*. He teaches at the University of North Texas.

DAVID FERRY (b. 1924) is a poet and a leading translator and scholar of Classical poetry in Latin and Greek. He has won both the Lenore Marshall Prize and the Ruth Lilly Poetry Prize.

GABRIEL FRIED (b. 1974) is the author of *Making the New Lamb Take* and editor of *Heart of the Order: Baseball Poems*.

ROBERT FROST (1874–1963) is the author of some of the most famous American poems ever written, including "Mending Wall" and "The Road Not Taken." He won an unprecedented four Pulitzer Prizes for his poetry, and was awarded the Congressional Gold Medal in 1960 for his poetical works.

ALICE FULTON (b. 1952), the daughter of a visiting nurse, is Professor of English at Cornell University. Her use of scientific metaphor has won her the Bobbitt Prize from the Library of Congress and many fellowships, including a Guggenheim Fellowship and a MacArthur Award.

BRENDAN GALVIN (b. 1938) won the Iowa Poetry Prize in 1997 for *Hotel Malabar*. His *Habitat: New & Selected Poems* (2005) was a finalist for the National Book Award.

SANDRA GILBERT (b. 1936), a professor at the University of California at Davis, is an important feminist scholar, critic and poet. Her collection *Kissing The Bread* won an American Book Award.

GREY GOWRIE (b. 1939) is a poet, critic, and anthologist, and also a Lord of the Realm, the hereditary Chief of Clan Ruthven. Gowrie was silent as a poet for many years until he underwent a cardiac transplant and wrote the poems that make up the newest parts of *Third Day: New and Collected Poems.*

GORDON GRIGSBY (b. 1927) is the author of three books of poetry, and the founding editor and publisher of *Evening Street Review.*

THOM GUNN (1929–2004), born in England, became a devoted Californian and one of the first modern poets to write openly and movingly about the Gay scene in San Francisco and the scourge of HIV. He won the Lenore Marshall Poetry Prize from the Academy of American Poets. Gunn died of acute polysubstance abuse, including methamphetamine.

RAMON GUTHRIE's (1896–1973) most renowned work, *Maximum Security Ward*, was about an intensive care unit. He died from bladder cancer and complications of its treatment.

ROBERT HASS (b. 1941) is one of the most influential and distinguished contemporary poets in America, as well as one of the country's most significant advocates of Japanese literature. He served as Poet Laureate from 1995–97, and won the National Book Award and the Pulitzer Prize for *Time and Materials.*

MARILYN HACKER (b. 1942) is one of the great political poets of our time, deeply involved with issues related to sexuality, Feminism, HIV and breast cancer. Her book *Presentation Piece* won the National Book Award. Her *Selected Poems* won The Poets' Prize in 1996. She is Professor of English at City College in New York City.

RACHEL HADAS (b. 1948) teaches at Rutgers University in New Jersey. Her memoir, *Strange Relation: A Memoir of Marriage, Dementia, and Poetry*, and many recent poems are about her husband's Alzheimer's Disease.

DONALD HALL (b. 1928) served as U.S. Poet Laureate from 2006–07. Many of his later poems concern illness, particularly the suffering and eventual death from leukemia of his wife, poet Jane Kenyon. He is also known for his writing on baseball and his essays on other poets. His many poetry collections include *The One Day*, which won the National Book Critics Circle Award and the *Los Angeles Times* Book Prize.

THOMAS HARDY (1840–1928), the author of *Tess of the D'Urbervilles* and many other renowned novels, is perhaps the only writer to be a great novelist in one century and a great poet in the next. Many of his best poems were written in mourning following the death of his first wife Emma in 1912. He died of pleurisy after dictating his final poem to his second wife.

ELIZABETH HARRINGTON (1947–2012) had a Ph.D. in psychology. Her poems on medical issues appeared in *Field, Nimrod* and *The Hudson Review*. She won the Allen Ginsberg Poetry Prize.

CLARINDA HARRISS (b. 1939) is a Professor of English at Towson University. The author of a number of poetry collections, she has recently published *The White Rail*, a book of stories, and co-edited *Hot Sonnets*, an anthology.

ROBERT HAYDEN (1913–1980) was born in Detroit and was a lifelong Michigan resident. He served as Consultant in Poetry to the Library of Congress from 1976–78. His *Collected Poems* was published in 2013.

TOM HEALY (b. 1961) is a writer, poet, and chairman of the Fulbright Foreign Scholarship Board. He is the author of two books, *Animal Spirits* and *What the Right Hand Knows*, which was a finalist for the 2009 *Los Angeles Times* Book Award and the Lambda Literary Award

SEAMUS HEANEY (1939–2013), Nobel Laureate in Literature, was the most important poet of Irish ancestry since Yeats, and perhaps the most important English-language poet of the past fifty years. His collection, *Human Chain*, was published posthumously.

WILLIAM ERNEST HENLEY (1849–1903) spent three years in hospital at The Old Infirmary, Edinburgh, and wrote most of his poems from his sick bed at age twenty-five while suffering from tuberculosis of the bone. The surgical pioneer Dr. Joseph Lister amputated Henley's leg, and Robert Louis Stevenson used Henley as the model for Long John Silver in *Treasure Island*. In addition to his collection, *In Hospital* (1888), Henley is the author of "Invictus," one of the most famous of all Victorian poems.

ZBIGNIEW HERBERT (1924–1998) was one of the most important Polish poets of the modern era and a distant relative of English poet George Herbert. He worked as a lice-feeder in a typhus institute during the German occupation of World War II.

BOB HICOK (b. 1960) is the author of seven books of poetry, including *Animal Soul*, a finalist for the National Book Critics Circle Award. He teaches at Virginia Tech University.

EDWARD HIRSCH (b. 1950) is one of America's most distinguished poets. He has won a MacArthur Fellowship, a Pulitzer Prize, and a National Book Critics Circle Award, and is President of the John Simon Guggenheim Memorial Foundation.

JANE HIRSHFIELD (b. 1953), a distinguished writer, is the author of seven books of poetry and a book of essays, *Nine Gates: Entering the Mind of Poetry*. She is a chancellor of the Academy of American Poets.

TONY HOAGLAND (b. 1953), author of four books of poetry, is winner of the James Laughlin Award, and the Mark Twain Humor Prize. He teaches at the University of Houston.

DANIEL HOFFMAN (1923–2013) wrote in a multiplicity of verse forms, including poetic riddles and an award-winning, book-length poem about William Penn's negotiations with Native Americans. From 1973–74, he served as Consultant in Poetry to the Library of Congress.

CYNTHIA MARIE HOFFMAN (b. 1975) is the author of two books of poems, *Sightseer*, winner of the Lexi Rudnitsky First Book Prize, and *Paper Doll Fetus*, a collection that gives voice to a variety of fantastical uterine inhabitants.

OLIVER WENDELL HOLMES (1809–1894) was the first significant physician-poet in America and one of the most popular writers of his day.

MIROSLAV HOLUB (1928–1998) was a physician-poet, perhaps the most important since William Carlos Williams. Born in Pilsen, Czechoslovakia, he was a forced laborer during the Holocaust and studied medicine after World War II. Having first achieved recognition as an immunologist, he began writing poetry at age thirty.

MARIE HOWE (b. 1950) is the author of three acclaimed collections of poetry, including *What The Living Do*, which recounts her brother's death from AIDS.

TED HUGHES (1930–1998) was one of the most eminent poets and translators of the twentieth century, the author of many best-selling books for both adults and children. He was appointed Poet Laureate of England in 1984, a post he held until his death, as well as to the Order of Merit, one of Britain's highest honors.

THOMAS JAMES (1946–1974) died at the age of twenty-seven, shortly after the first publication of his only book, *Letters to a Stranger*.

KIMBERLY JOHNSON (b. 1971), a poet and scholar, is the author of three collections, most recently *Uncommon Prayer*, and a translator of Virgil's *Georgics*.

DONALD JUSTICE (1925–2004) was one of the preeminent American poets of the second half of the twentieth century. He was awarded the Pulitzer Prize for his *Selected Poems*, and received the Bolligen Prize for Poetry in 1991.

WELDON KEES (1914–1955) lived in New York as painter, poet, critic and jazz musician. In 1955, his car was found on the Golden Gate Bridge; no one saw him jump and his body was never recovered.

JANE KENYON (1947–1995) wrote movingly of her battles with depression and leukemia. She was poet laureate of New Hampshire at the time of her death.

KATE KIMBALL (b. 1981), originally from Salt Lake City, recently earned her MFA from Virginia Tech University.

TED KOOSER's (b. 1939) unvarnished poetry from the American heartland earned him a Pulitzer Prize for *Delights and Shadows*. He was Poet Laureate from 2004–05. Like Wallace Stevens, he worked as an executive in the insurance industry.

PHILIP LARKIN (1922–1985), a notorious misanthrope, worked as a librarian and as a jazz critic. He was offered the Poet Laureateship of England in 1984 but declined for health reasons. Larkin died of esophageal cancer.

D. H. LAWRENCE (1885–1930) wrote poems, plays, short stories, and literary criticism, and also painted. He was a pioneer of British Modernism and wrote almost 800 poems.

DENISE LEVERTOV (1923–1997), born and raised in Ilford, Essex, married an American and came to the United States in 1947. She came under the influence of William Carlos Williams. Politics and war were major poetic subjects. Levertov was poetry editor at *The Nation*. She died of lymphoma.

PHILIP LEVINE (b. 1928) was born and raised in working-class Detroit, where he worked in the auto plants. He has won two National Book Awards and the Pulitzer Prize, and served as Poet Laureate of the United States from 2011–12.

HENRY WADSWORTH LONGFELLOW (1807–1882) was for many years America's most popular poet, whose most celebrated works include "Paul Revere's Ride", *The Song of Hiawatha*, and *Evangeline*.

ROBERT LOWELL (1917–1977) was the most honored American poet of his generation and founder of the Confessional School. The youngest ever Poetry Consultant to the Library of Congress, he won the National Book Award and the National Book Critics Circle Award, and twice won the Pulitzer Prize. He suffered greatly with bipolar disorder and alcohol.

THOMAS LUX (b. 1946), acclaimed poet and teacher, is the recipient of the Kingsley Tufts Prize in poetry and the holder of the Bourne Chair at Georgia Tech University. Fascinated by medical technology, Lux has written many poems on medical subjects.

EDGAR LEE MASTERS (1868–1950), once one of America's favorite poets, is known for his *Spoon River Anthology*, one of the most popular books of poetry ever written.

WILLIAM MATTHEWS (1942–1997) was one of the most influential and beloved poets of the generation that came to maturity in the 1960s and 1970s. His *Time & Money* won the National Book Critics Circle Award. He died of a heart attack.

JANE MAYHALL (1918–2009) published a number of works of poetry, fiction, and drama. Her collection of poems, *Sleeping Late on Judgement Day*, which reflected her grief following the death of her husband, brought her much acclaim at the age of 85.

J. D. McCLATCHY (b. 1945) is a poet, literary critic, and editor, as well as America's most important librettist. He is editor of the *Yale Review* and president of the American Academy of Arts and Letters.

JO McDOUGALL (b. 1935) is a poet of the Arkansas delta and its small towns. She is the author of five books of poetry and a memoir.

GARDNER McFALL (b. 1952) is the author of two books of poems, *The Pilot's Daughter* and *Russian Tortoise*, and two children's books. She is also the author of the libretto of *Amelia*, which premiered at the Seattle Opera in 2010.

JAMES MERRILL (1926–1995) won every major poetry prize: the Pulitzer Prize, the Bollingen Prize, The National Book Critics Circle Award, the inaugural Bobbitt Prize from the Library of Congress, and the National Book Award (twice). He established the Ingram Merrill Foundation. Merrill died from an AIDS-related heart attack.

JOSEPHINE MILES (1911–1985), born in Chicago, was tutored at home because of her disabling arthritis. Her *Collected Poems 1930–1983* won the Lenore Marshall Poetry Prize.

A. A. MILNE (1882–1956) was a noted author and playwright, especially beloved for his children's books *Winnie the Pooh* and *The House at Pooh Corner*, and his two books of children's verse *When We Were Very Young* and *Now We Are Six*.

JOHN MILTON (1608–1674), was the canonical author of *Paradise Lost* and other essential works of English literature. The probable onset of glaucoma led to total blindness by 1654. He then dictated his work to several amanuenses, one of whom was Andrew Marvell. Milton died of kidney failure.

LADY MARY WORTLEY MONTAGU (1689–1762) was an aristocrat and writer of letters and poems. In 1715 she survived an attack of smallpox; she later helped introduce the Turkish practice of inoculation. Her husband was ambassador to Istanbul, and she wrote one of the first significant Western books on Islamic culture.

LISEL MUELLER (b.1924) was born in Germany and lives in Lake Forest, Illinois. Her eight collections of poems include *Alive Together: New & Selected Poems*, which won the Pulitzer Prize, and *The Need to Hold Still*, which received the National Book Award.

LES MURRAY (b.1938) is Australia's most honored contemporary poet, renowned for his comic yet cosmic verse. He has won the T. S. Eliot Prize and was given the Queen's Gold Medal for Poetry.

OGDEN NASH (1902–1971), America's master of light verse, was born in Rye, New York but spent most of his life in Baltimore. He worked as an ad-man and collaborated with S.J. Perelman and Kurt Weill on *One Touch of Venus*. He died of Crohn's Disease at Johns Hopkins University Hospital.

THOMAS NASHE (1567–c.1601) was a satirist who wrote polemics and the first picaresque novel. Though plague, food poisoning, and stroke have been suggested, the cause of his death is unknown.

HOWARD NEMEROV (1920–1991), an eminent poet, won the National Book Award, the Pulitzer Prize, and the Bollingen Prize for *The Collected Poems of Howard Nemerov*. He is the only poet to have served as both Poetry Consultant to the Library of Congress and its reincarnation, Poet Laureate.

ALICE NOTLEY (b.1945) has written over twenty-five books of poetry, including *Mysteries of Small Houses*, which won the *Los Angeles Times* Book Award; *Disobedience*, awarded the Griffin International Poetry Prize; and *Grave of Light: New and Selected Poems 1970–2005*, which received the Lenore Marshall Poetry Prize.

DENNIS NURKSE (b. 1949), the son of Nazi refugees, is a renowned contemporary surrealist and a humanitarian. He has won fellowships from both the National Endowment for the Arts and the Guggenheim Foundation. Nurkse currently teaches at Sarah Lawrence College, after many years giving workshops at Rikers Island.

ALICIA SUSKIN OSTRIKER (b. 1937), a poet and scholar, has written the most outstanding poems on breast cancer and body image. Her philosophical reflections on aging, *The Book of Seventy*, received a Jewish National Book Award.

OVID (Publius Ovidius Naso, 43 BCE– 17/18 CE) ranks with Virgil and Horace as one of the three canonical poets of Latin literature. He is best known for three sets of erotic verse and *The Metamorphoses*, a mythological hexameter poem. Among his shorter works is the *Medicamina Faciei Femineae*, devoted to the treatment of dermatological conditions and feminine cosmetics.

LINDA PASTAN (b. 1932), a former Poet Laureate of Maryland, writes frequently on medical subjects; many of her immediate family members are physicians. She won the 2003 Ruth Lilly Poetry Prize.

ROBERT PINSKY (b. 1940) served as U.S. Poet Laureate from 1997–2000. He is an acclaimed teacher and translator, the poetry editor of *Slate*, and the head of the graduate poetry program at Boston University. He won the Lenore Marshall Poetry Prize for *The Figured Wheel*.

SYLVIA PLATH (1932–1963), acclaimed poet and novelist, is one of the best and most powerful poets of the Confessional generation. Deeply interested in doctors and hospitals, she wrote many poems on those subjects.

STANLEY PLUMLY (b. 1939) is a powerful, plain-spoken formalist of the Mid-West and an important scholar, of Keats especially. His writing has often dealt with the demons of mental and physical illness. Plumly directs the creative writing program at the University of Maryland, College Park. In 2009, he was named Maryland's Poet Laureate.

RAINER MARIA RILKE (1875–1926), one of the most significant poets in the German language, Rilke (like Kafka) was born in Prague and deeply influenced by modern painting and sculpture. His *New Poems* were written while serving as Rodin's secretary. Rilke's leukemia was diagnosed just before his death.

E. A. ROBINSON (1869–1935) was raised in Gardiner, Maine, referred to as Tilbury Town in his poems. He won three Pulitzer Prizes for his poetry, and was a favorite poet of Theodore Roosevelt, who gave him a stipend. "How Annandale Went Out" (included herein) is the earliest poem on euthanasia.

KAY RYAN (b. 1945) was Poet Laureate of the United States from 2008 to 2010. Her book, *The Best Of It: New & Selected Poems* won the Pulitzer Prize.

MICHAEL RYAN (b. 1946) is the author of *Threats Instead of Trees*, a finalist for the National Book Award; *In Winter*, a National Poetry Series selection; *God Hunger*, which received the Lenore Marshall Poetry Prize; and *New and Selected*

Poems, which received the Kingsley Tufts Poetry Award. He teaches at the University of California at Irvine.

MARY JO SALTER (b. 1954), an acclaimed formalist, teaches in the Writing Seminars program at The Johns Hopkins University. She is the author of many books of poetry and drama, the longtime editor of the *Norton Anthology of Poetry*, and the former poetry editor of *The New Republic*.

GRACE SCHULMAN (b. 1935) is the author of six books of poetry and distinguished professor of English at Baruch College (CUNY). She served as the poetry editor of the *Nation* from 1972 to 2006, and directed the 92nd Street Y Poetry Center from 1973 to 1985.

FREDERICK SEIDEL (b. 1936) is the author of a number of acclaimed books of poetry. He was once referred to as "the poet the twentieth century deserved."

VIJAY SESHADRI (b. 1954) recently won the Pulitzer Prize for *3 Sections*. He also won the James Laughlin Award for *The Long Meadow*. He currently directs the graduate nonfiction program at Sarah Lawrence College.

ANNA SEWARD (1742–1809), a Romantic poet and famous letter-writer, was often called the Swan of Lichfield. After her death, three volumes of letters and poems were published, introduced by Sir Walter Scott.

ANNE SEXTON (1928–1974), a poet and children's book author, was a student with Sylvia Plath and John Starbuck in Robert Lowell's famed course at Boston University. She wrote a number of poetry collections, including *Live or Die*, for which she won the Pulitzer Prize. A member of the Confessional generation, she wrote several poems of medical interest. Sexton suffered mental illness most of her life and ended a suicide.

WILLIAM SHAKESPEARE (1564–1616) is the supreme literary figure in the English language. His gravestone is inscribed with a curse against moving his bones.

HARVEY SHAPIRO (1924–2013), served in many prominent editorial positions at the *New York Times*, including editor of the Book Review from 1975–1983. His books include *The Sights Along the Harbor: New & Collected Poems*.

JASON SHINDER (1955–2008) died of lymphoma and leukemia. The last of his three books, *Stupid Hope*, is about his final illness. Shinder was a devoted teacher and the Poet Laureate of Provincetown, Massachusetts.

ANYA SILVER (b. 1968) teaches an interdisciplinary course on medicine and the humanities at Mercer University. Many of the poems in her prize-winning book, *The Ninety-Third Name of God*, are about her battle with breast cancer.

LOUIS SIMPSON (1923–2012), editor, translator, and literary critic, won the Pulitzer Prize for *At The End of The Open Road*.

L. E. SISSMAN (1928–1976) was an ad man and lived in Boston. His frank response to his prolonged clinical course and oncoming death from Hodgkin's Disease is included in his book *Night Music*.

FLOYD SKLOOT (b. 1947) is a distinguished poet and memoirist. Many of his recent books deal with his personal recovery from a viral disease of the nervous system.

TOM SLEIGH (b. 1953) is the author of a number of poetry collections, including *Space Walk*, winner of the Kingsley Tufts Award. Other honors include an Academy Award from the American Academy of Arts and Letters and the Shelley Award from the Poetry Society of America. He teaches in the MFA Program in Creative Writing at Hunter College.

LEE SLONIMSKY (b. 1952) is a sonneteer, mathematician, and venture capitalist—a pioneer in the development of hedge funds dedicated to social concerns.

WILLIAM JAY SMITH (b. 1918) is the author of many books for adults and children. He was Poetry Consultant to the Library of Congress from 1968–70.

MARC STRAUS (b. 1945) is a distinguished oncologist, art collector, gallerist, and poet. His verse play *Not God* has been performed Off Broadway.

WALLACE STEVENS (1879–1955) is among the most influential American poets, a pillar of Modernism. He worked at an insurance company in Hartford and composed many poems while out walking. His *Harmonium* (1921) is perhaps the most important first book of the 20th century. Stevens died of stomach cancer.

ROBERT LOUIS STEVENSON (1850–1894), Scottish novelist, poet, essayist, and travel writer, is the author of *Treasure Island, Kidnapped*, and *A Child's Garden of Verses*. Whether from tuberculosis, bronchiectasis, or sarcoidosis, Stevenson suffered with chest disease all his life. He died in the South Pacific.

JOHN STONE (1936–2008), a cardiologist, served as Associate Dean at the Emory School of Medicine in Atlanta. A kind and caring doctor, his medical experiences permeate his poetry. He died of cancer.

RUTH STONE (1915–2011), author of thirteen books of poetry, was the recipient of numerous honors, including the National Book Award, the National Book Critics Circle Award, and the Shelley Memorial Award.

TERESE SVOBODA (b. 1950) is an innovative poet, memoirist, and fiction writer, the author of many books in and across genres.

WISŁAWA SZYMBORSKA (1923–2012), born in Prowent, Poland, Szymborska has a relatively small published corpus of 250 short poems filled with existential puzzles and philosophical import. She received the Nobel Prize in Literature in 1996.

JAMES TATE (b. 1943) is one of the most prominent practitioners of the prose poem. His *Selected Poems* won the Pulitzer Prize and *Worshipful Company of Fletchers* won the National Book Award. He teaches at the University of Massachusetts, Amherst.

HENRY DAVID THOREAU (1817–1862), the author of *Walden*, was a fine poet, who expressed the American character in Nature's realm.

BRIAN THORNTON (b. 1975) teaches at the University of Kurdistan and lives in Iraq.

ELLEN BRYANT VOIGT (b. 1943) is the pioneering founder of the low-residency MFA concept and the MFA program at Warren Wilson College. Her books have been finalists for the National Book Award and the National Book Critics Circle Award.

JENNIFER WALLACE (b. 1954) teaches poetry and urban ecology at the Maryland Institute College of Art in Baltimore and an editor at *The Cortland Review*.

ROSANNA WARREN (b. 1953), poet, critic, and editor, is the winner of numerous fellowships. Her collection, *Stained Glass*, was the Lamont Selection. She is Hanna Holborn Gray Distinguished Service Professor at the University of Chicago.

FLORENCE WEINBERGER (b. 1932) is the author of four collections, most recently *Sacred Graffiti*. The Holocaust has been a major theme in her work.

WALT WHITMAN (1819–1892) served as a volunteer nurse in the American Civil War and memorialized his experiences in *Drumtaps*, the book that preceded *Leaves of Grass*. Whitman's singing line became the basis for contemporary free verse; he remains modern poetry's most influential progenitor.

RICHARD WILBUR (b. 1921) has twice won the Pulitzer Prize, as well as the National Book Award and every other major poetry prize, and has served as Poetry Consultant to the Library of Congress. He is also known for his translations of French plays by Molière, Racine, and Corneille; his poems for children; and the lyrics he contributed to Leonard Bernstein's *Candide*.

C. K. WILLIAMS (b. 1936) is the acclaimed author of numerous collections of poetry, including *The Singing*, which won the National Book Critics Circle Award, and *Repair*, which won the Pulitzer Prize. He teaches in the creative writing program at Princeton.

WILLIAM CARLOS WILLIAMS (1883–1963) was the most important physician-poet since Keats and the most revolutionary figure in free verse since Whitman. A general practitioner and pediatrician in Rutherford, New Jersey, Dr. Williams often wrote his poems while making rounds. Because of his own infirmities he served only one year of his term as Poetry Consultant to the Library of Congress.

WILLIAM WORDSWORTH (1770–1850) initiated the Romantic era through his injection of the personal and conversational. His first book was co-authored with Samuel Coleridge, *Lyrical Ballads*, after which Wordsworth continued to be productive for many years. His "emotion recollected in tranquility" has remained the implicit motto of most artists ever since.

WILLIAM BUTLER YEATS (1865–1939) was an Irish poet, playwright, and political polemicist. He is widely regarded the greatest poet of the 20th century and the most important poet in English since Keats a century before.

C. DALE YOUNG (b. 1969) is a poet and radiation oncologist who lives in San Francisco. He also teaches in the Warren Wilson low-residency MFA program.

INDEX OF POETS

ACKNOWLEDGEMENTS

Thanks to the following rights-holders for permission to reprint as indicated:

Dannie Abse, "Pathology of Colours," "The Stethoscope," and "In the Theatre" from *New Selected Poems: 1949–2009*, Anniversary Collection. Copyright © 1977, 2009 by Dannie Abse. Reprinted by permission of Sheep Meadow Press and The Random House Archive & Library. "Song for Pythagoras" from *White Coat Purple Coat: Collected Poems 1948–1988*. Copyright © 2003 by Dannie Abse. Reprinted by permission of George Braziller, Inc.

Dick Allen, "Agoraphobia." Reprinted with the permission of the author.

Yehuda Amichai, "When I Have a Stomach Ache" and "A Pity. We Were Such a Good Invention," translated by Assia Gutmann, from *The Selected Poems of Yehuda Amichai*, edited and translated by Stephen Mitchell and Chana Bloch. Copyright © 1992 by Stephen Mitchell and Chana Bloch. Reprinted by permission of the University of California Press.

Philip Appleman, "Eulogy" from *New and Selected Poems, 1956–1996*. Copyright © 1996 by Philip Appleman. Reprinted with the permission of The Permissions Company, Inc., on behalf of the University of Arkansas Press, www.uapress.com.

Elizabeth Arnold, "Heart-Valve" from *Poetry* (July/August 2010). Reprinted with the permission of the author.

W. H. Auden, "Give me a doctor" from *Selected Shorter Poems, 1927–1957*. Copyright © by 1966 by W. H. Auden. Used by permission of Random House, an imprint of The Random House Publishing Group, a division of Random House LLC. All rights reserved.

Coleman Barks, excerpt from "Body Poems" from *Winter Sky: New and Selected Poems 1968–2008*. Copyright © 1972, 2008 by Coleman Barks. Reprinted by permission of The University of Georgia Press.

Charles Baudelaire, "Anywhere Out of the World" from *Paris Spleen: Little Poems in Prose*, translated by Keith Waldrop. Copyright © 2009 by Keith Waldrop. Reprinted by permission of Wesleyan University Press.

Gottfried Benn, "Little Aster," translated by Scott Horton, from *Harper's Magazine* (August 12, 2007). Reprinted with the permission of the translator. "Zeh was a Pharmacist," translated by Michael Hofmann, from *Impromptus: Selected Poems and Some Prose*. Originally in *Poetry* (November 2009). Translation copyright © 2013 by Michael Hofmann. Reprinted by permission of Farrar, Straus & Giroux, LLC.

David Bergman, "My Father's Penis," "A Child's Garden of Curses," and "The Beauty of Convalescence." Reprinted with the permission of the author.

John Berryman, #67 ["I don't operate often"] and #235 ["Tears Henry shed"] from *The Dream Songs*. Copyright © 1969 by John Berryman. Reprinted by permission of Farrar, Straus & Giroux, LLC.

Elizabeth Bishop, "Visits to St. Elizabeths" from *The Complete Poems 1927–1979*.

1979, 1983 by the President and Fellows of Harvard College. Reprinted by permission of The Belknap Press of Harvard University Press.

Sharon Dolin, "Stroke" from *Realm of the Possible*. Copyright © 2004 by Sharon Dolin. Reprinted with the permission of The Permissions Company, Inc., on behalf of Four Way Books, www.fourwaybooks.com.

Mark Doty, "The Embrace" from *Sweet Machine*. Copyright © 1998 by Mark Doty. Reprinted by permission of HarperCollins Publishers.

Stephen Dunn, "The Routine Things Around the House" from *New and Selected Poems 1974–1994*. Copyright © 1984 by Stephen Dunn. Used by permission of W. W. Norton & Company, Inc. Dunn, "Plaisir" from Poetry (July/August 2008). Reprinted with the permission of the author.

T. S. Eliot, "Hysteria" from *The Complete Poems and Plays 1909–1950*. Reprinted by permission of Faber & Faber, Ltd.

Claudia Emerson, "Anatomical Model" and "The Polio Vaccine, Chatham, Virginia, 1964" from *Figure Studies*. Copyright © 2008 by Claudia Emerson. "Migraine: Aura and Aftermath" and "The X-Rays" from *Late Wife*. Copyright © 2005 by Claudia Emerson. All reprinted with the permission of Louisiana State University Press.

William Empson, "Missing Dates" from *The Complete Poems*. Copyright © William Empson. Reprinted by permission of Curtis Brown, Ltd.

Daniel Mark Epstein, "The Good Doctors" from *The Glass House: New Poems*. Copyright © 2009 by Daniel Mark Epstein. Reprinted with the permission of Louisiana State University Press.

B. H. Fairchild, "Flight" from *The Arrival of the Future*. Copyright © 2000 by B. H. Fairchild. Reprinted with the permission of The Permissions Company, Inc., on behalf of Alice James Books, www.alicejamesbooks.org.

David Ferry, "At the Hospital" from *Of No Country I Know: New and Selected Poems and Translations*. Copyright © 1993, 1999 by David Ferry. Reprinted by permission of The University of Chicago Press.

Gabriel Fried, "The Circumcision" from *Making the New Lamb Take*. Copyright © 2007 by Gabriel Fried. Reprinted with the permission of The Permissions Company, Inc., on behalf of Sarabande Books, Inc, www.sarabandebooks.org.

Alice Fulton, "Claustrophilia" from *The New Yorker* (August 2, 2010). Copyright © 2010 by Alice Fulton. Reprinted by permission of Brandt & Hochman Literary Agents, Inc. All rights reserved.

Brendan Galvin, "Fear of Gray's Anatomy" from *Habitat: New and Selected Poems 1965–2005*. Copyright © 1977, 2005 by Brendan Galvin. Reprinted with the permission of Louisiana State University Press.

Sandra M. Gilbert, "Colonoscopy Sonnet" from *Poetry* (May 2008). Reprinted with the permission of the author.

Grey Gowrie, "The Third Day" from *Third Day, New and Selected Poems*. Copyright © 2008 by Grey Gowrie. Reprinted by permission of Carcanet Press, Ltd.

Gordon Grigsby, "Dying Together" from *Tornado Watch* (Columbus: The Ohio State

Jane Hirshfield, "A Hand" from *Given Sugar, Given Salt*. Copyright © 2001 by Jane Hirshfield. Reprinted by permission of HarperCollins Publishers.

Tony Hoagland, "Lucky" from *Donkey Gospel*. Copyright © 1998 by Tony Hoagland. Reprinted with the permission of The Permissions Company, Inc., on behalf of Graywolf Press, www.graywolfpress.org.

Daniel Hoffman, "Brainwaves" from *The Center of Attention*. Copyright © 1974 by Daniel Hoffman. Reprinted with the permission of the Estate of Daniel Hoffman. "A Triumph" from *A Little Geste: And Other Poems*. Copyright © 1960 by Daniel Hoffman, Reprinted with the permission of Louisiana State University Press.

Miroslav Holub, "Casualty" and excerpt from "Interferon" from *Poems Before and After: Collected English Translations*. Reprinted by permission of Bloodaxe Books, Ltd.

Cynthia Marie Hoffman, "Miscarriage" from *Paper Doll Fetus*. Copyright © 2014 by Cynthia Marie Hoffman. Reprinted by permission of Persea Books, Inc. All rights reserved.

Marie Howe, "Pain" from *What the Living Do*. Copyright © 1997 by Marie Howe. Used by permission of W. W. Norton & Company, Inc.

Ted Hughes, "Fever" from *Birthday Letters*. Copyright © 1998 by Ted Hughes. Reprinted by permission of Farrar Straus & Giroux, LLC and Faber & Faber, Ltd.

Thomas James, "Fever," "Mummy of Lady Named Jemuteseonekh," and "Snake Bite" from *Letters to a Stranger*. Copyright © 1973 by Thomas James. Reprinted by permission of Houghton Mifflin Harcourt Company. All rights reserved.

Kimberly Johnson, "Ode on My Belly Button" and "Ode on My Episiotomy" from *A Metaphorical God*. Copyright © 2009 by Kimberly Johnson. Reprinted with the permission of Persea Books, Inc. All rights reserved.

Donald Justice, "Counting the Mad" from *New and Selected Poems*. Copyright © 1960, 1967, 1987 by Donald Justice. Used by permission of Alfred A. Knopf, an imprint of the Knopf, Doubleday Publishing Group, a division of Random House, LLC. All rights reserved.

Jane Kenyon, "Otherwise" from *Otherwise: New and Selected Poems*. Copyright © 1996 by Jane Kenyon. Reprinted with the permission of The Permissions Company, Inc., on behalf of Graywolf Press, www.graywolfpress.org.

Kate Kimball, "Transfusion." Reprinted with the permission of the author.

Ted Kooser, "The Urine Specimen" from *Flying at Night: Poems 1965–1985*. Copyright © 2005 by Ted Kooser. Reprinted by permission of the University of Pittsburgh Press.

Philip Larkin, "Faith Healing," "Heads in the Women's Ward," and "The Building" from *Collected Poems*. Copyright © 2012 by The Estate of Philip Larkin. Reprinted by permission of Farrar, Straus & Giroux, LLC.

D. H. Lawrence, "Sick" and "Healing" from *The Complete Poems of D. H. Lawrence*, edited by Vivian de Sola Pinto and F. Warren Roberts. Copyright © 1964, 1971 by Angelo Ravagli and C. M. Weekley, Executors of the Estate of Frieda Lawrence Ravagli. Used by permission of Penguin Group (USA) Inc.

Denise Levertov, "Talking to Grief" from *Poems 1972–1982*. Copyright © 1978 by Denise Levertov. Reprinted by permission of New Directions Publishing Corp.

Phlip Levine, "Night Thoughts over a Sick Child" from *On the Edge* (Second Press, 1963). Reprinted with the permission of the author.

Dennis Nurkse, "Things I Forgot to Tell My Doctor" from *Rules of Paradise*. Copyright © 2001 by Dennis Nurkse. Reprinted by permission of The Permissions Company, Inc., www.fourwaybooks.com

Alicia Ostriker, "Nude Descending" from *The Little Space: Poems Selected and New 1968–1998*. Copyright © 1998 by Alicia Ostriker. Excerpt from "The Mastectomy Poems" from *The Crack in Everything*. Copyright © 1996 by Alicia Ostriker. "Lymphoma" from *The Book of Seventy*. Copyright © 2009 by Alicia Ostriker. All reprinted by permission of the University of Pittsburgh Press.

Ovid, excerpt from "The Art of Beauty" from *The Love Books of Ovid*, translated by J. Lewis May (London: The Bodley Head, 1925).

"At the Gynecologist's" from *Carnival Evening: New and Selected Poems 1968–1998*. Copyright © 1994 by Linda Pastan. Used by permission of the publisher W. W. Norton & Company, Inc.

Robert Pinsky, excerpt from "Essay on Psychiatrists" from *Sadness and Happiness*. Copyright © 1975 by Princeton University Press, renewed 2003. Reprinted by permission of Princeton University Press. "Dying" from *The Figured Wheel: New and Collected Poems 1966–1996*. Copyright © 1996 by Robert Pinsky. Reprinted by permission of Farrar, Straus & Giroux, LLC.

Sylvia Plath, "Two Views of a Cadaver Room" from *The Colossus and Other Poems*. Copyright © 1959 by Sylvia Plath. Used by permission of Faber and Faber, Ltd., and Alfred A. Knopf, an imprint of the Knopf, Doubleday Publishing Group, a division of Random House, LLC. All rights reserved. "Thalidomide" and "The Surgeon at 2 a.m." "Face Lift" and "In Plaster" from *The Collected Poems*, edited by Ted Hughes. Copyright © 1959 by Sylvia Plath. Copyright © 1965, 1971, 1981 by the Estate of Sylvia Plath. Reprinted by permission of HarperCollins Publishers, Inc. and Faber & Faber, Ltd.

Stanley Plumly, "The Iron Lung" from *Now That My Father Lies Down Beside Me: New and Selected Poems 1970–2000*. Copyright © 2000 by Stanley Plumly. Reprinted by permission of HarperCollins Publishers. "Cancer" from *The New Yorker* (July 12, 2010). Reprinted with the permission of the author.

Rainer Maria Rilke, "Going Blind" from *The Essential Rilke*, translated by Galway Kinnell and Hannah Liebmann. Translation copyright © 1999 by Galway Kinnell and Hannah Liebmann. Reprinted by permission of HarperCollins Publishers.

Kay Ryan, "Tired Blood" from *Niagara River*. Copyright © 2005, 2010 by Kay Ryan. "Bitter Pill" from *The Best of It: New and Selected Poems*. Copyright © 2005, 2010 by Kay Ryan. Both used by permission of Grove/Atlantic, Inc.

Michael Ryan, "A Good Father" and "TV Room in the Children's Hospice" from *New and Selected Poems*. Copyright © 2004 by Michael Ryan. Reprinted by permission of Houghton Mifflin Harcourt Publishing Company. All rights reserved.

Michael Salcman, "Dr. Williams Delivers a Baby" from *The Clock Made of Confetti*. Copyright © 2007 by Michael Salcman. "The Apprentice Surgeon" from *The Enemy of Good is Better*. Copyright © 2011 by Michael Salcman. Both poems reprinted with the permission of Orchises Press. "Medulloblastoma" from *Rhino* (2013). Reprinted with the permission of the author.

Mary Jo Salter, "Half a Double Sonnet" from *Sunday Skaters*. Copyright © 1994 by Mary

Jo Salter. Used by permission of Alfred A. Knopf, an imprint of the Knopf, Doubleday Publishing Group, a division of Random House, LLC. All rights reserved.

Grace Schulman, "Query" and "Walk!" from *The Broken String*. Copyright © 2007 by Grace Schulman. Reprinted by permission of Houghton Mifflin Harcourt Publishing Company. All rights reserved.

Frederick Seidel, "Dune Road, Southampton," "At New York Hospital," "Doctor Love," and "Holly Andersen" from *Poems 1959–2009*. Copyright © 2009 by Frederick Seidel. Reprinted by permission of Farrar, Straus & Giroux, LLC. Farrar, Straus & Giroux, LLC

Vijay Seshadri, "Nursing Home" from *3 Sections*. Originally published in *Plume*. Copyright © 2013 by Vijay Seshadri. Reprinted with the permission of The Permissions Company, Inc., on behalf of Graywolf Press, www.graywolfpress.org

Anne Sexton, "Doctors" and "The Double Image" from *The Complete Poems*. Copyright © 1960 by Anne Sexton, renewed © 1988 by Linda G. Sexton. Reprinted by permission of Houghton Mifflin Harcourt Publishing Company. All rights reserved.

Harvey Shapiro, "6/20/97" from *The Sights Along the Harbor: New and Collected Poems*. Copyright © 2001 by Harvey Shapiro. Reprinted by permission of Wesleyan University Press.

Jason Shinder, "How I Am," "Ocean," and "Arrow Breaking Apart" from *Stupid Hope*. Copyright© 2005, 2009 by the Estate of Jason Shinder. Reprinted with the permission of The Permissions Company, Inc., on behalf of Graywolf Press, www.graywolfpress.org.

Anya Silver, "To My Body" from *The Ninety-Third Name of God*. Copyright © 2010 by Anya Krugovoy Silver. Reprinted with the permission of Louisiana State University Press. "Leaving the Hospital" from *New Ohio Review* (Spring 2011). Reprinted with the permission of the author.

Louis Simpson, "Typhus" from *The Owner of the House: New Collected Poems 1940–2001*. Copyright © 2003 by Louis Simpson. Reprinted with the permission of The Permissions Company, Inc., on behalf of BOA Editions Ltd., www.boaeditions.org

L. E. Sissman, "Negatives" and "A Deathplace" from *Night Music*. Copyright © 1999 by The President and Fellows of Harvard College. Reprinted by permission of Houghton Mifflin Harcourt Publishing Company. All rights reserved.

Floyd Skloot, "The Onset of Vertigo" from *Notre Dame Review* (Summer/Fall 2010): 124. Copyright © 2010 by Floyd Skloot. "Sway" from *The Hopkins Review* 3.3 (2010): 317–318. Copyright © 2010 by Floyd Skloot. Both reprinted with the permission of the author. "Channel" from *Floyd Skloot: Selected Poems: 1970–2005*. Copyright © 2007 by Floyd Skloot. Reprinted with the permission of Tupelo Press.

Thomas Sleigh, "Clinic" from *Space Walk*. Copyright © 2007 by Thomas Sleigh. Reprinted by permission of Houghton Mifflin Harcourt Publishing Company. All rights reserved.

Lee Slonimsky, "Schema" from *Money and Light* (Austin, Tex.: SRLR Press, 2006). Copyright © 2006 by Lee Slonimsky. Reprinted with the permission of the author.

William Jay Smith, "A Picture of Her Bones" from *The World Below the Window: Poems 1937–2007*. Copyright © 1966 by William Jay Smith. Reprinted with the permission of the author.

John Stone, "Cadaver," "Talking to the Family," and "Getting to Sleep in New Jersey" from *Music from Apartment 8: New and Selected Poems*. Copyright © 1972, 2004 by John Stone. Reprinted with the permission of Louisiana State University Press.

Ruth Stone, "Healing" from *What Love Comes To: New and Selected Poems*. Copyright © 2010 by Ruth Stone. Reprinted with the permission of The Permissions Company, Inc., on behalf of Copper Canyon Press, www.coppercanyonpress.org.

Marc Straus, "Luck" from *Not God: A Play in Verse*. Copyright © 2006 by Marc J. Straus. Published 2006 by TriQuarterly Books/Northwestern University Press. Previously published in One Word (Evanston, Ill.: TriQuarterly Books/Northwestern University Press, 1994). All rights reserved.

Terese Svoboda, "Hysterical Leg" from *Weapons Grade*. Copyright © 2009 by Terese Svoboda. Reprinted with the permission of The Permissions Company, Inc., on behalf of the University of Arkansas Press, www.uapress.com. "Village Doctor." Reprinted with the permission of the author.

Wisława Szymborska, "Advertisement" from *Poems: New and Collected 1957–1997*. Copyright © 1995, 2000 by Wisława Szymborska. Reprinted by permission of Houghton Mifflin Harcourt Publishing Company. All rights reserved.

James Tate, "On the Subject of Doctors" from *Selected Poems*. Copyright © 1976 by James Tate. Reprinted by permission of Wesleyan University Press.

Brian Thornton, "Losing Lars Degener." Reprinted with the permission of the author.

Ellen Bryant Voigt, "Damage" from *Claiming Kin*. Copyright © 1976 by Ellen Bryant Voigt. Reprinted by permission of Wesleyan University Press.

Jennifer Wallace, "Tumor" from *Desire Path* by Myrna Goodman, Maxine Silverman, Meredith Trede, and Jennifer Wallace (Chappaqua, New York: Toadlily Press, 2005). Reprinted with the permission of the author.

Rosanna Warren, "Aftermath" from *Ghost in a Red Hat*. Copyright © 2007 by Rosanna Warren. Used by permission of W. W. Norton & Company, Inc.

Florence Weinberger, "Getting in Bed with a Man Who is Sick" from *Carnal Fragrance*. Copyright © 2004 by Florence Weinberger. Reprinted with the permission of Red Hen Press, www.redhen.org.

Richard Wilbur, "To His Skeleton" from *Collected Poems 1943–2004*. Copyright © 2004 by Richard Wilbur. Reprinted by permission of Houghton Mifflin Harcourt Publishing Company. All rights reserved.

William Carlos Williams, "The World Contracted to a Recognizable Image" from *The Collected Poems of William Carlos Williams, Volume II, 1939–1962*, edited by Christopher MacGowan. Copyright © 1962 by New Directions Publishing Corporation. Reprinted by permission of New Directions Publishing Corp.

C. Dale Young, "Sepsis" from *Torn*. Copyright © 2011 by C. Dale Young. Reprinted with the permission of The Permissions Company, Inc., on behalf of Four Way Books, www.fourwaybooks.com.